Klee

Klee

A STUDY OF HIS LIFE AND WORK BY
GUALTIERI DI SAN LAZZARO

Frederick A. Praeger, Publishers
NEW YORK · WASHINGTON

TRANSLATED FROM THE ITALIAN BY STUART HOOD

FIRST PUBLISHED IN THE UNITED STATES OF AMERICA IN 1957 BY
FREDERICK A. PRAEGER, INC., PUBLISHERS
111 FOURTH AVENUE, NEW YORK 3, N.Y.

LIBRARY OF CONGRESS CATALOG CARD NUMBER 57-11232

FIRST PUBLISHED IN THIS FORMAT, 1964
REPRINTED 1965
PRINTED IN GREAT BRITAIN BY JARROLD & SONS LTD, NORWICH

Contents

WE ARE GRATEFUL TO

M. FELIX KLEE

AND THE KLEE FOUNDATION, BERNE

FOR INVALUABLE ASSISTANCE IN THE PREPARATION OF THIS BOOK

OUR THANKS ARE ALSO DUE TO THOSE WHO

PERMITTED US TO PHOTOGRAPH

THE WORKS OF KLEE IN THEIR COLLECTIONS

AND PARTICULARLY TO

M. AND MME BÜRGI OF BERNE,

MLLE ANGELA AND M. SIEGFRIED ROSENGART OF LUCERNE,

MR. F. C. SCHANG AND MR. BERGGRUEN

SELF-PORTRAIT—DRAWING FOR A WOODCUT. 1909.

The Little Arab

The son of a Swiss mother and a German father, Paul Klee was a wonderful epitome of the physical and psychological characteristics of both his parents. It would be difficult—indeed almost impossible—to be more German and yet more Swiss than he. But some distant trace of the Mediterranean had left its mark on him both physically and spiritually. In photographs taken when he was a child, he has the secretive, sensual face of a little Arab. As an adult he was always to feel strongly the lure of the Mediterranean. The thin line of the beard running straight from the corners of his mouth, his thick lips and dark, penetrating eyes are characteristically African. And because of this remote influence which has never been accurately defined by

1

LANDSCAPE—from a sketchbook. *c. 1898. Klee-Stiftung, Berne.*

his biographers—his family on his mother's side is suspected of North African connections—he was himself to become African. From Africa came the mystery, the incantation which seemed to be the source of his last works.

His biographers tell us that his mother, Ida Maria Klee, came from Basle, which is at once the most bitingly witty and the most sensual of Swiss cities. His father, Hans, on the other hand, was German. A common passion for music had brought the couple together—that and Hans Klee's almost legendary powers of sarcasm, which a native of Basle could not but consider with a certain benevolent tolerance.

Paul was born on 18th December 1879, at Münchenbuchsee near Berne where his father—he had had to give up singing—taught as a schoolmaster. Tempered by the understanding of the

ARCO—SOUTH TYROL. 1896. *Felix Klee Collection, Berne.*

boy's mother, the sarcasm of Hans Klee became humour in his son. The musical aspirations of the parents reappeared undiminished in Paul who was even tempted at one stage to give up the violin, to which he owed his first childish successes, and by devoting himself to singing, realize the most tenacious of his parents' desires.

There was another child of the marriage—Mathilde, whose portrait by Klee is well known (Cat. 3). But she had no influence on her brother although she was devoted to him. Heredity, upbringing and his own personality made an artist of Klee. In his case his need to escape was merely an extension of his personality and not the expression of a revolt against the milieu in which he lived, as it was in the case of many other artists.

In a 'sous-verre' by his son, Hans

3

VIRGIN IN A TREE. 1903.

Klee has the majestic vanity of a Grand Elector (page 6). But in the photographs of the same period he displays the simple cordiality of an emaciated, bearded patriarch. Perhaps he was a bit of both. But few patriarchs have had the good fortune to bring into the world a more affectionate and devoted son. Even more than a father Hans Klee must have been a friend to his son. It was to his father that the young art student later confided his first ambitions as an artist and in enthusiastic letters expressed the sincere ambitions awakened within him by the masterpieces of the Munich Pinakothek.

This sarcastic man then, was his son's first playfellow—the first admirer of the drawings which the child, encouraged by his maternal grandmother, produced with his left hand. Not that he was really left-handed—that we know from his son, Felix Klee. He drew and painted with the left hand but

STILL LIFE—FLOWERPOTS AND VASES. 1908. *Klee-Stiftung, Berne.*

PORTRAIT OF MY FATHER. 1906. *Felix Klee Collection, Berne.*

wrote with the right. He could also write and draw with both hands simultaneously, working either from right to left or from left to right. For heavy work he preferred to use the left hand.

The small boy's other friends were the cats which held absolute sway over the district of Berne to which his family had moved shortly after he was born. And to the cats, too, Klee was to remain loyal all his life. He would never be able to do without them. They were to occupy the same place in his work as Picasso at a certain period gave to the owl—perhaps an even more important place, for to Picasso the owl is merely a symbol of antiquity, whereas the cat is Klee's most familiar demon, the genius of his hearth. At school his gay, ironic character won him the liking of his companions—particularly of those who were most dissatisfied

PORTRAIT OF LILY KLEE. 1906. *Felix Klee Collection, Berne.*

with its very broad education, which took no account of individual leanings. Klee was one of the most pugnacious of the boys, yet he never showed any desire to assume the authority of leader. His notebooks were full of drawings with which he was continually busy as he followed the lesson with one ear. But in the Greek class he was more attentive, for Greek appealed to the poet in him.

The Klee archives contain twelve notebooks from these years, full of drawings which cannot be described as masterpieces but which have nevertheless sensibility. The most moving are those from his early childhood on themes presumably suggested by his grandmother—the Christ child, a guardian angel, the Christmas-tree. The Christmas-tree was to revert to being a simple pine and become one of his most constant symbols—the leafy symbol which, after his journey to Tunisia, he was to set against the full round moon of the South. The boy was particularly fond of processions in which men and animals alternated. Certain spidery personages which were to reappear later in the illustrations to *Candide* are already there. There is a certain humour, too, in these early drawings but it disappears in later works which reveal his growing preoccupation with technicalities. Space and light are the two problems which beset the young artist. But he is still moved by love and his youthful landscapes from the years 1895 and 1896 show sensibility and sometimes technical ability worthy of a mature artist. One remembers with particular emotion an envelope which at the age of ten he painted and cut out as if it were

BERNE—INDUSTRIAL QUARTER WITH CATHEDRAL TOWER. 1909. *Klee-Stiftung, Berne.*

IN THE QUARRY. 1913. *Klee-Stiftung, Berne.*

a real letter from a fount of type. It is already a miniature Klee. Many years later he was to return to the same theme in the famous drawing *The Spirit of the Letter*. He was very fond of flowers and plants, of birds and butterflies and of fish with human features, such as he was to come across later in the Aquarium at Naples. Like a true botanist, he knew both the German and Latin names of the flowers. He loved to draw and paint cyclamens, gentians and Alpine roses. Unlike his drawings of birds, which are copied from books, those of flowers are very delicate—not scholastic exercises but precious preliminary studies by an artist with a precise feeling for colour.

When he left school after taking his final examination, he inserted an advertisement in the student magazine, to which he had been a faithful contributor, offering "a large number of Madonnas, of Mary Magdalenes, of girls, brigands, etc., taken from the notebooks of a sixth-form pupil".

He drew whatever came into his head—Madonnas, Mary Magdelenes

9

BIRDCAGE ON THE COLUMN. 1908. *Klee-Stiftung, Berne.*

and brigands. But other things too of which his mother one day disapproved. Like many boys of his age, Paul Klee was greatly taken up with the problem of sex. He himself records in his Diary that he was attracted by the beauty of small girls at a precocious age and that he had even wanted to be a girl so as to be able, like them, to wear lace-frilled knickers. His first love—at the age of seven—was a little Italian girl. Some years later he was strongly attracted by a cousin from Basle in whose house he stayed in the autumn of 1887 and 1888. Finally a drawing of a naked woman with her belly full of children fell into his mother's hands. The poor woman, whose ignorance of sex education was

HANNAH. 1910. F. C. Schang Collection, New York.

complete, was terrified and reacted with such severity as to produce inevitably the opposite effect from that intended. From that moment only whatever was prohibited could attract the adolescent boy. His studies left him indifferent, apart from Greek poetry and music which, along with drawing, were his great passions. He wrote erotic poetry and erotic stories which he immediately destroyed. But the study of landscape and life in the open air gave his tormented spirit a certain peace and allowed him—as we have said—to express himself artistically and produce works which even today are worthy of our admiration.

It was natural, therefore, that having passed his examinations with no great distinction, he should decide to study painting seriously. In 1898 he left for Munich. He was nineteen years old.

YOUNG WOMAN IN A DECK CHAIR. 1909. *Klee-Stiftung, Berne.*

HUMAN WEAKNESS. 1913. *Klee-Stiftung, Berne.*

MUNICH—THE STATION. 1911.

Three Years of Darkness

Of the three years which Paul Klee spent in Munich studying painting, first at Professor Knirr's and later at the Academy under Stück, we have only the artist's account together with some rather insignificant works. Klee was not to find himself until he had calmed both his senses and his imagination, thanks to the beneficial influence of Lily, a young pianist who eight years later was to become his wife.

Evidently there was no lack of accommodating, maternal girls in Munich, but his first attempts were disappointing, precisely because of the motherly attitude which they felt they must assume towards this inexpert

provincial. The young man examined himself and realized that he loved none of them; he was simply attracted by the mystery of the female species. None of them succeeded in filling the void in his heart.

Yet these years had a decisive influence on his future. It was at Munich that he found confidence in himself, analysing every inclination with a subtlety, with a pedantry even, worthy of a psychiatrist. Music, literature and painting attracted him equally. But he did not leave it to chance to decide whether he was to be a musician, writer or painter. He chose painting because he had a definite feeling that painting, more than music or poetry, would allow the full expression of his personality. "I shall make painting take steps forward'', he wrote to his parents in Berne. The rigorous self-discipline which he imposed on himself had occasionally amusing results, as when he entered in a notebook the names of all the girls he had not yet possessed. The last name in the list is that of Lily, beside which he wrote the one word: "Wait".

While he waited for Lily, who was to be the woman in his life, a poor girl enabled him to satisfy the most urgent promptings of his sexual curiosity. She was far from being his ideal woman—an imaginary creature to whom he had given the name of Eveline—but she was at least a being of the opposite sex. One evening he got drunk. He thought of Lily and felt guilty, but he justified himself by arguing that he did not yet belong to any one woman. His instincts were polygamous, yet even in his moments of depression—they were due chiefly to sexual frustration—he was sure of one thing: that painting was his real profession. It was a conviction which grew in him. In the autumn of 1900 he was at last allowed to join Professor Stück's class at the Academy. Although he thought he had by now a fair mastery of draughtsmanship Klee had to admit that colour was a difficult obstacle. And Stück—as Kandinsky was to say, for he too was a

"MAKE WAY, MAKE WAY, FOR THE REVEREND COLONEL" (CANDIDE),

pupil of this wretched academic painter —was a poor ally in the struggle.

He consoled himself in Lily's company. She for her part succeeded in inviting him to her house on Christmas Eve. While continuing his sexual initiation with other girls, Klee was more and more attracted to the young pianist with whom he shared his passion for music. Music and poetry were his great comfort. He composed and wrote verses in honour of his imaginary Eveline. Literature, too, attracted him. Tolstoy's *Resurrection* overwhelmed him and he had no peace until Lily too had read it; for more and more he felt the need to gain the approval of a girl whom he already considered his fiancée. Yet from time to time he was tortured by jealousy and feared he might be mistaken in his choice. "It would be a pity", he wrote in his Diary, "because Lily has a good influence on me."

At school he was increasingly confident although Stück did not share his opinion and even encouraged him to leave painting and take up sculpture.

In the spring of 1901, he felt he could lay down a guiding principle for his life: "First of all, the art of living; then as my ideal profession, poetry and philosophy, and as my real profession, plastic art; in the last resort, for lack of income, illustrations."

He was attracted by the satirical journals; but he realized that his ambitions went much deeper. One day he

SKETCH OF A STREET IN A TOWN. 1912. *Klee-Stiftung, Berne.*

16

ANATOMY OF APHRODITE. 1915. *Felix Klee Collection, Berne.*

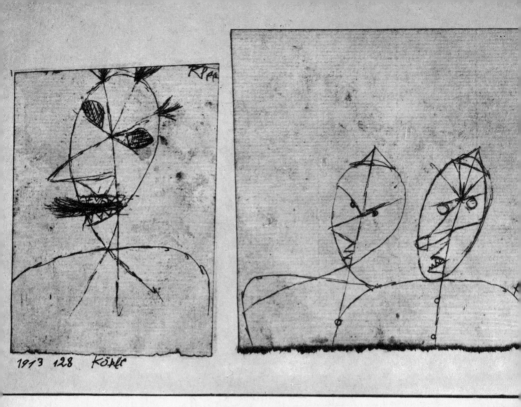

HEADS. 1913. *Klee-Stiftung, Berne.*

decided to be a great portrait painter. "It is not my task to reproduce appearances", he notes in his Diary, "for that there is the photographic plate—I want to penetrate into the inmost meaning of the model. I want to reach the heart. I write words on the forehead and round the lips. But my faces are truer than life." Many years later he kept his promise and succeeded in expressing a reality which is no longer only physical without being merely psychological. But he still had only a vague presentiment of that reality. Although they were expressed with such confidence,

his ambitions were actually more modest. Gradually his erotic fancy seemed to be assuaged. In his heart there was a growing need for a "noble" love. At Whitsun, which he was spending with Lily's parents—her father who was a doctor had treated him for a nervous disorder of the heart some months previously—he was able to win a first but decisive victory over the young pianist. From that day, Lily was prepared, in order to marry him, to wait the eight years he thought necessary to reach his full artistic maturity.

Klee undoubtedly had a lengthy adolescence and a tortuous development. His three years in Munich were dark years lit from time to time by a ray of light. When he went home to Berne in the summer of 1901 and prepared to set out for Italy with his friend Haller, whom he had known since he was six, and who had been with him in Munich, he was cured. He could at last think that "he had become a moral man—even from the point of view of sex". The three years in Munich had not been wasted. They would have been so perhaps had he not met Lily, from whom he had been able to part for the moment without pain. "Now I have staked everything on Italy." Italy, too, like Lily, was to have a beneficial effect on him. Italy was to be his convalescence; after the troubled years in Munich he was, for the first time, sure of himself.

A FRAGMENT OF EDEN. 1913. *F. C. Schang's Collection, New York.*

LITTLE PORT. 1914. *Felix Klee Collection, Berne.*

LITTLE VIGNETTE FOR EGYPT. 1918. *Felix Klee Collection, Berne.*

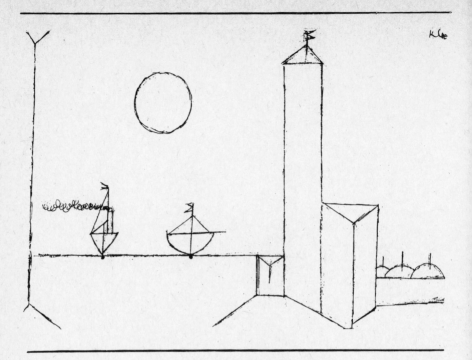

TOWER BY THE SEA. *Klee-Stiftung, Berne.*

Mastering Life

Women apart, and with them he had no contact, Paul Klee's Italy is like Stendhal's—entirely composed of theatres and museums. But whereas Stendhal abandoned himself to his impulses, to his unflagging zest for things Italian, Klee severely observed and analysed his feelings. To him the most important thing in Italy was his own reactions. This does not mean to say that he did not allow himself to be carried away by enthusiasm, but immediately afterwards he noted the effects which that enthusiasm had produced in his mind. Paul Klee was interested principally in Paul Klee and the flowering of his own personality— the way in which his moral and artistic conscience developed. The sub-title of his Diary could well be: How I Became Paul Klee.

In Italy, as in Munich, and as later in Paris, Africa, Germany and Egypt, he was seeking himself. Italy gave him the opportunity of measuring himself against antiquity, of confronting the academic art they had taught him at Munich with Classicism, towards which he had been steered by Burckhardt's famous book, although he did not always agree with it. His sense of his own unimportance did not frighten him, for his future was always present in his mind. He did not hesitate to say that he had reached the point where he could lump together Antiquity and Renaissance. "But I cannot conceive", he adds immediately, "any artistic relationship with our own epoch. And the creation of anything outside the framework of our age seems very suspect to me." Naturally, since he knew nothing of French art, he could have only the vaguest idea of his own age.

In October 1901 then, Paul accompanied by his friend, Hermann Haller, crossed the frontier. In Milan, he admired the Tintorettos in the Brera; but Genoa was his first real stopping-place in Italy. His first port, his first sea, his

first voyage in a steamer (to Leghorn, which he found boring): all these he saw like pictures in an exhibition. Compared to Genoa, which he described as a "dramatic" city, Rome, the goal of his journey, suggested to his imagination the epithet "epic". Some months later he was to tire of Rome and prefer Naples; but his first contact, celebrated with generous libations in an *osteria*, aroused his spirits and his senses.

He found lodgings in the Via dell' Archetto. With his precious Burckhardt under his arm he at once began to visit museums and churches. The Sistine Chapel and the frescoes of Pinturicchio and Raphael left the pupil of Knirr and Franz von Stück bewildered, as if he had been the victim of a vigorous and unmerited assault. But Michelangelo's *Pietà* left him indifferent. And for the Baroque he con-

THE FLOWER AS OBJECT OF LOVE. 1915. *Klee-Stiftung, Berne.*

ZOO. 1918. *Klee-Stiftung, Berne.*

24

ceived something approaching hatred. On the other hand his enthusiasm was aroused by the Byzantine mosaics of San Giovanni in Laterano and by certain sculptures "in a primitive style", whose beauty lay entirely in expression. The emotion awakened in him by these sculptures was to be more fruitful than the assault inflicted on him in the Sistine Chapel. By the time that he was really Paul Klee, Michelangelo and Raphael were to be eclipsed however by Leonardo, who was already—even if unconsciously—his ideal. But the primitive arts would always be dear to his heart. If the *Laocoön* annoyed him the *Belvedere Apollo* fascinated him. It was with difficulty that he accepted Guido Reni's *Beatrice Cenci*.

At the Museo Nazionale in Naples he admired the frescoes from Pompeii which seemed to have been "painted and discovered" for him. In the Aquarium his enthusiasm was kindled by the starfish, the octopuses and the great shell-fish, which he describes as "expressive". "Expressive" is an adjective which frequently recurs in his vocabulary. In the ordinary octopuses he finds a comic resemblance to art dealers. One of them, in particular, seemed to look at him as if he were a new Boecklin.

Not only did the Aquarium at Naples, many years later, inspire some of his most beautiful compositions, but certain effects of light, certain submarine tones, certain delicate iridescent passages have a strict connection with that distant revelation. Unlike Picasso, Klee never exploited his own sensations immediately. He allowed them to mature slowly within himself. Almost

25

CATS. 1915. *Klee-Stiftung, Berne.*

all Klee's 'personages', like the sea-anemones and shell-fish in the Aquarium at Naples, would one day have their individual atmosphere, removed from which they could not conceivably exist. A fish in an aquarium, in a bowl or even caught in a net, a bird in a cage, a man shut up in a room or on a stage —all Klee's poetry lies in magic limitation of this kind, what we might call the enchantment of acclimatization. We can already at this date establish that the starting-point of his work was almost always a gently satirical observation. One composition on which he worked in Rome was called *Moralizing on squint Chimneys*. The work is valueless but in the title there is the germ of the picture—all Klee is there already. Speaking of another satirical composition showing a group of three young men, he says he hopes to succeed one day in creating not only with the mind but beauty too. This hope was to be fulfilled with the years.

In the evening he went to the opera,

CHILD. 1918. *Klee-Stiftung, Berne.*

DRAWING FOR SALOME. 1920. *Siegfried Rosengart Collection, Lucerne.*

to concerts and the theatre. Once, on entering a theatre and finding himself surrounded by women, he had the painful impression of reliving one of his childhood dreams. From Munich Lily wrote to ask his impressions of Roman women. Paul was not a new Stendhal and had not made the acquaintance of a single one. The only women with whom he passed a pleasant evening were two friends from Berne whom he met by chance in Florence. Rome was not Munich. The girls of easy virtue did not like artists; they preferred cavalry officers and moved in different circles.

The great Duse drew from him a severe critical judgment with which Stendhal would have disagreed. But Réjane, who was making a triumphant tour of Italy, filled him with en-

29

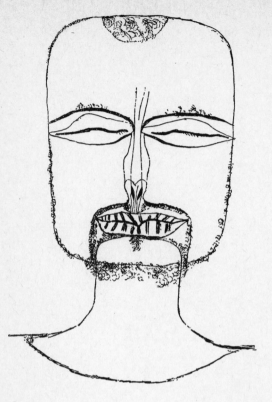

thusiasm—perhaps because she reminded him of a girl with whom he used "to play games that made him happy". But the great actress left him with a great sadness in his heart which was dispelled some days later by another Parisian actress—one who did not come from the legitimate stage, la Belle Otero. She had a poor voice but posed delightfully and was a woman in every inch of her body. Even Cléo de Merode, whom he saw some time later, could not make him forget her.

Music continued to excite him but he did not neglect literature, passing from Plato to Zola, from Tolstoy to Tacitus. Goethe, whom he discovered in Italy and some of whose works he read over and over again was "the only bearable German". He was a German such as he himself would have liked to be. Goethe and Lily gave Klee to Germany. To the young artist, who was still totally ignorant of French art— shortly before leaving Rome he saw an exhibition of French art and admired some drawings by Rodin and Forain— France, in spite of its fascination,

seemed a country without a future.

In April 1901, sad and listless, he left Rome after a last visit to the Borgia apartments in the Vatican—"the most beautiful thing the Renaissance gave Rome" —to see the Pinturicchio frescoes.

In Florence he now felt sure enough of his own judgments and did not hesitate to express them very boldly. Thus he described Botticelli as a better colourist than Titian. He was not mistaken, however, in considering Veronese superior to Titian as far as colour was concerned. He admired the Raphael portraits and Cranach's *Eve.*

In the Museo Nazionale he was particularly attracted by Donatello, but the Gothic, being more "expressive", aroused a stronger emotion.

It was another man who returned to Berne in May 1902, after seven months' absence. In spite of the fringed beard which he had allowed to grow in honour of the men of antiquity, he was no longer Pan among the reeds. He was a man who wanted to 'climb stairs'— really climb. From now on he had only one ambition—to master life.

DREAM LANDSCAPE WITH CONIFERS. 1920. *Private Collection, Berne.*

The Artist Alone

To master life meant above all not to allow himself to be diverted from his path. After his return to Berne, Klee earned a little money by playing the violin in the town orchestra, by giving music and drawing lessons. Later, in Munich, after his marriage to Lily, he was servant, cook and nursemaid to his own family; but both there and in Berne he dominated life—refusing to be distracted from his own work and following his own path to the end.

Between 1902 and 1906 he made notable technical progress in his art. So much must be recognized, although it is difficult to share his enthusiasm for his early etchings, in which he unfortunately lapses into Teutonic grotesque. The engravings, and later the 'sous-verres', gave him the opportunity of grappling with the problem of line, with which one day he would be able to express all his poetry.

Let us concede, then, that he had—as he claimed—discovered his style although he had in fact merely dis-

THE TIGHTROPE WALKER. 1923. *Klee-Stiftung, Berne.*

covered how to engrave a zinc plate or a piece of glass. The important thing was that he should be aware of his internal processes. He himself said that his immediate and at the same time most distant goal was to harmonize the architectonic sense (which he had learned to understand in Italy) with his own sense of poetry, which had lately undergone profound modifications. From being tenderly lyrical it had become bitterly satirical. "I protest", he wrote in his Diary.

Did A Virgin in a Tree (page 4), which Stück managed to get exhibited some years later in the 'Sezession' of 1906, along with other etchings, really merit the severity with which the critics treated it? Not certainly for the reasons adduced by one critic who reproached the crack-brained artist with producing a "mad anatomy" of things. Although the feeling of these etchings: A Virgin in a Tree, Comedian, A Man grovelling before the Crown, Woman and Beast, Menacing Head (Cat. 5) is still grotesque, in some of them—like Two Men meet: Each supposing the other to be of Higher Rank (Cat. 2)—the aim is pleasingly satirical and not unworthy of comparison with Gogol, on whom Klee nourished his own sense of

DEPARTURE FOR THE VOYAGE. 1920. *Private Collection, Berne.*

FANTASTIC ARCHITECTURE WITH THE RIDER. 1918. *Klee-Stiftung, Berne.*

humour. *The Hero with one Wing*—one of the first works that Klee sold—for 300 marks, a high figure for those days—has a rhymed comment by the painter, and in the comment, if not in the engraving itself, we find Klee's real sense of humour, which had been stimulated by the Wright brothers' attempt at flight.

In short, Klee did not so much anticipate his own taste—this he did very occasionally in the 'sous-verres'—as synthesize in his etchings and 'sous-verres' the taste represented by Hodler (whom he did not admire), by Blake and by Beardsley, whose works he knew. If in the etchings he had to face up to the problem of line, the 'sous-verres', which were produced by etching with a needle on a piece of glass coated with black or coloured paints and printing it on paper gave him training for the alchemy of the future and forced him to respect the delicate play of tones. One example is the delicate *Garden Scene with a Watering Can* (1905, Cat. 7), which has a surprising French charm.

35

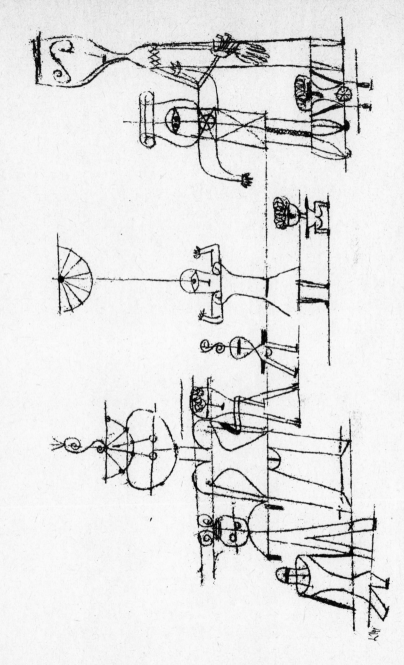

↑ LET HIM KISS ME WITH THE KISS OF HIS MOUTH (from the Song of Songs). 1921. *Angela Rosengart Collection, Berne.*

EXOTICS' THEATRE. 1922. *Klee-Stiftung, Berne.*

MIRACULOUS LANDING. 1920. *Klee-Stiftung, Berne.*

During these years, too, he acquired his taste for variations. The theme of father and son suggested a whole series of works: A *Father with his Son*, A *Father seen by his Son*, A *Father blessing his Son*. But they were not as successful as he wished and he destroyed them. "Only the titles remain", he summed up philosophically in his Diary.

He was not aware, meanwhile, of the disorderly way in which he was acquiring a culture. "I heard 'Bajazzo' before 'Hänsel and Gretel', saw Sudermann's plays before seeing Ibsen and Ibsen before seeing Hebbel . . . Amiet before van Gogh."

Although sometimes he had to admit that his work was not going well, at other times he unhesitatingly stated that he had succeeded in forcing nature to conform to his style. "Everything becomes Klee", he said. Everything was Klee already—but only in intention, as we see from his description of a work in progress: "Water—on the water waves—on the waves a boat—on the boat, a woman—on the woman, a man I invented in the summer of 1904. A precarious construction."

He made some trips to Munich to clear up his position *vis-à-vis* the military authorities, to see Lily again and to "kiss youth on the mouth before it is too late". Then he made a flying visit to Berlin where the critic Heilbut attempted in vain to arrange an

DRAWING FOR "PLANTS, EARTH AND KINGDOM OF THE AIR". 1920. *Klee-Stiftung*,

exhibition of his drawings and have some published in various periodicals. Occasionally Lily visited him in Berne; clearly he no longer nourished a morbid passion for her. He had had a glimpse of the abyss in the bitter years of adolescence and had no desire to relive the burden of those distant days. But without her affection, which he no longer doubted, he would not have been so sure of himself. Unfortunately the girl's father was not very happy about their relationship and the two young people had frequently to meet in secret.

Music, literature and new friends, comforted the young man's solitude. He tended to let friends give him advice, but if he saw that their paths diverged did not hesitate to break with them, however great the help he had received from them in the past.

On 31st May 1905 he was able— along with his friends Moilliet and Bloesch—at last to realize one of his most cherished dreams: a short, mere fortnight's trip to Paris. The journey was not decisive. Klee was not yet mature enough to take stock of modern art with that resolution he had shown when faced with classical art in Italy. It was his first visit to a country which, being still too much of a German, he could not but regard with an unconscious element of distrust. He visited the Louvre, the Luxembourg Museum which was at that time the gallery of modern art, and the main sights of the town. In the evening he went to theatres, to *bals musettes* and to cafés. La Comédie-Française, l'Opéra-Comique, le Bal Bullier, la Taverne de

40

LANDSCAPE WITH YELLOW BIRDS. 1923. *R. Doetsch-Benziger Collection, Basle.*

l'Olympia—all these he visited. His greatest joy was to rediscover Leonardo and to admire the fine Corots in the Louvre. He seemed less enthusiastic about the moderns, with the exception of Renoir. In Puvis de Chavannes he recognized the artist who had been the first to influence Hodler. He was pleased to discover Spanish influences —of Velasquez and of the Goya he loved—in Manet. Monet he found unequal because impulsive, but rich in talent. Sisley—refined, Pissarro—dry. In Carrière, who was closer to his own problems, he saw a good example of how to deal with tonality.

Such coolness on his part is disappointing. It hardly seems possible that he did not hear people speak of Cézanne, whom he was not to discover until some years later in Munich and in

him recognize his master. The truth is that Klee was too great an admirer of the German mind to find fruitful models in France. "I have nothing to learn from the French", he writes in his Diary. It was only some years later that he realized that the problems which were besetting him were precisely those which the French had so daringly attempted to resolve.

Meanwhile he had completed his study of anatomy by taking classes with Professor Strasser in Berne. There he no longer found the work boring, as he had in Munich, where only the consoling thought that the knowledge he was acquiring might some day prove useful had encouraged him to continue.

He read a good deal. He copied out the whole of the *De Profundis* by Wilde, from whom he had learned that art is a

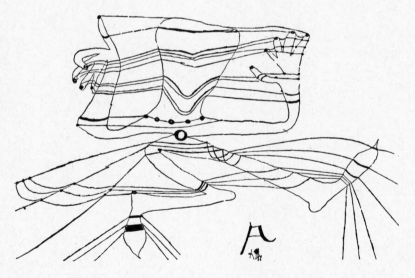

DANCE OF THE VEIL. 1920. *Ibach Collection, Barmen.*

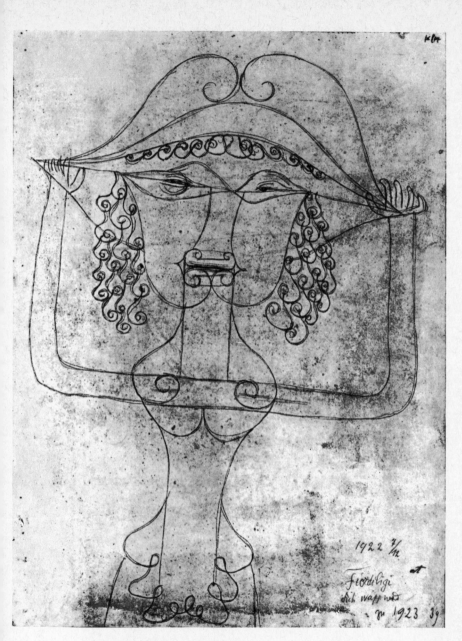

FIORDILIGI. 1923. *Angela Rosengart Collection, Lucerne.*

space and symbolism. Reading was like a fever; but he kept his finger on his pulse. "Yesterday I would have refused to read *The Portrait of Dorian Gray*, which today amuses me and the day before yesterday would have intoxicated me." Voltaire's *Candide*, which he felt the urge to illustrate some years later, affected him deeply. Naturally he did not miss concerts. He was present at one concert by Casals (whom he considered the best musician who had ever lived) which was something of a fiasco, because Casals found the players below any acceptable standard and refused to continue. These two passions—music and literature—reinforced Klee's Germanic sentiments.

As his feelings became more clearly defined and insisted on finding artistic expression, the desire grew in him to live in a large town. "For Lily, too, it will be a good idea to leave her parents' home. We shall work together—for how long I don't know."

At last, at the beginning of September 1906, he overcame the resistance of the girl's father and was able to announce his engagement officially. The marriage took place at Berne on the 16th and some weeks later, in October, he was already living in a *pension* in Munich with his wife. Soon after they moved to a small second-floor flat looking on to a courtyard. Lily gave piano lessons and Klee, who had so long sighed for his solitude to come to an end, caught himself writing in his Diary: "I live alone in a city of five thousand painters."

THE OPERA-BOUFFE. 1925. *Mrs. Charlotte Purcell's Collection, Chicago.*

44

SENECIO. 1922. *Kunstmuseum, Basle.*

GROTESQUES FROM THE CIRCUS. 1925.
F. C. Schang Collection, New York.

Bonne à tout faire

"In the little flat in Munich," so the artist's son, Felix Klee tells us, "my mother practised her profession every day. She gave music lessons from morning to night and her husband, still the unknown artist, had to see to the chores and look after the baby. The little kitchen was his room; there his pictures and drawings saw the light, there glass was etched, photographs developed, nappies washed and socks mended. . . . In that same kitchen he made me wonderful toys with great skill—toy trains, a cardboard railway station and a puppet theatre. The heads were clay, the costumes cut and sewn by himself, the scenery pasted and painted. A careful record was kept of the family's income and expenditure, new pictures catalogued, a diary kept in which everything was entered down to my temperature and my progress in learning to speak. . . . In the afternoons my father took me to the outskirts of the town—he, furnished with a folding chair, an easel, a box of colours and a bottle of water; I, with some of my toys. For the summer holidays the whole family left for Berne to stay with my grandparents, or for Beatenberg where a great-aunt kept a hotel."

Perhaps the boy who wanted to be a little girl and wear frilled knickers was being punished by fate. In the Klee's small flat the roles of man and woman were reversed.

It is impossible to separate Klee's life from his work. Nothing in his life was lost to his art—everything he ever saw would one day find a place in his

THE CHILD. 1924. *F. C. Schang Collection, New York.*

work. Even during these first hard years in Munich his will-power and discipline allowed him to "master life" and every moment of these years became his.

Yet before Felix's birth on 30th November 1907 complicated things, Klee had had the good fortune to paint the portrait of the son of a chemist from Basle and that of Frau von Sinner for 800 marks in all.

He was, besides, not so much alone in the city of five thousand painters as he had thought in a moment of depression. He found old friends again and made new ones. He visited exhibitions and went to theatres and concerts. His greatest pleasure was that at home he could play music with Lily and other friends. But for the financial straits it might have been the life he was to lead later when he was at the Bauhaus in Weimar and Dessau. All of it remained imprinted on his mind. Will

47

DANCE OF THE SAD CHILD. 1921. *Klee-Stiftung, Berne.*

Grohmann rightly points out in his authoritative work on Klee that, more than ten years later, he immortalized two singers from the Bavarian State Opera, conducted by Bruno Walter, in *Fiordiligi* (page 43) and *The Voice-Cloth of the Singer Rosa Silber.*

Undoubtedly he was a disconcerting man. It is surprising how, sometimes, he does not have adequate technical ability to match the intense fervour of his mind. His genius seems to be buried deep down within him. Some years had to pass before he could break through to it. If Pablo Picasso with his immediate reactions is one pole of modern art, Paul Klee undoubtedly represents the opposite pole. We have to wait patiently for years before we discover in his work that architectural sense which had illumined his journey to Italy. Bad initial influences made the young artist lose a number of precious

years, but they were not entirely without their use, for they forced him to think things out and ponder them long. It is only in 1911, in the illustrations to *Candide* (published in 1920), that we recognize in him the great artist he was to become during the war. Yet from time to time there are highlights in his work of these years: the *Garden Scene with a Watering Can* of 1905, the delicious *Flower-girl with spots of Colour*, and the delicate *Youthful male head with blue eyes.* (Cat. 8, 9).

It was during the course of this long search for himself that he elaborated his complex theories. He is like a plant —a tropical one at that—which before putting out foliage puts down firm roots. Even the bad influences at the beginning of his career contributed to make Klee a unique artist. "Evil", he writes in his *Creative Confessions*, "will be neither a triumphant nor a pitiful

48

FRAGMENT FROM A BALLET FOR AEOLIAN HARP. 1922. *Angela Rosengart Collection, Lucerne.*

HERON. 1924. *F. C. Schang Collection, New York.*

50

AQUARIUM WITH SILVERY BLUE FISHES. 1924. *Private Collection, Berne.*

enemy, but a force which the totality will absorb.''

His first years in Munich—from 1905 to 1912—were years of novitiate and of fruitful encounters with the Impressionists, with Toulouse-Lautrec, Ensor, van Gogh, Cézanne and Kandinsky. But it differed from the novitiate in Berne with its excessive enthusiasms, which had been due perhaps to his desire to inspire Lily with his own faith in the future, for she was not an artist, was several years older than he, and hesitated to face life with a poor young man. The tone of the Diary is now less impulsive, more balanced. His faith in himself is not so much weakened as tempered by a gentle melancholy.

51

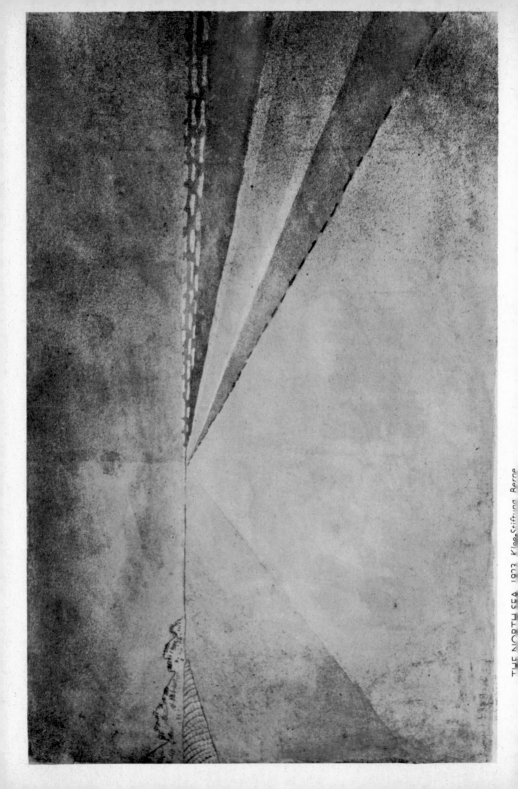

THE NORTH SEA. 1923. Klee Stiftung, Berne.

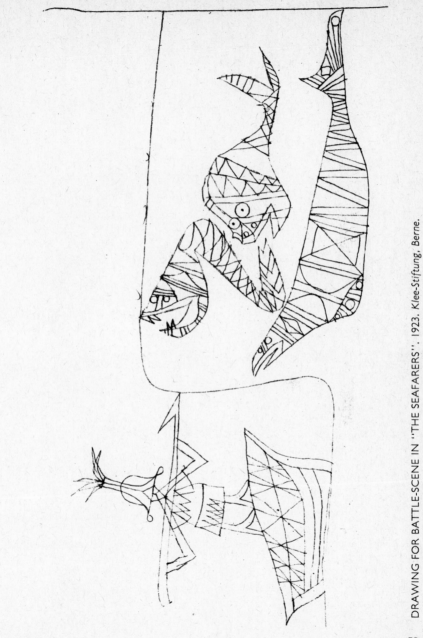

DRAWING FOR BATTLE-SCENE IN "THE SEAFARERS". 1923. Klee-Stiftung, Berne.

53

CONCERT ON THE TWIG. 1921. *Klee-Stiftung, Berne.*

To earn some money he considered contributing to *Simplizissimus*, the satirical review published in Munich, which—like the periodical *Jugend*—did much to help the spread of the "Modern Style". He therefore offered some of his drawings but they were not accepted and Klee, in any case, refused to adapt himself to the directives of the paper. For many years to come he would have no other way of mastering life except this—to refuse any compromise with his conscience. Instead he accepted for some months a modest post teaching art in an evening school.

54

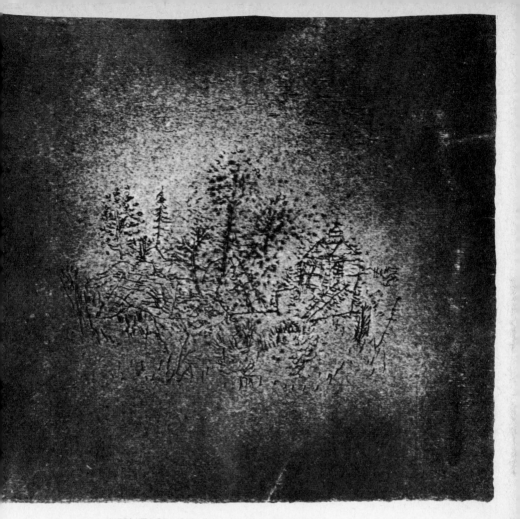

HERMITAGE. 1925. *Felix Klee Collection, Berne.*

The birth of Felix and domestic worries, did not prevent him from attending the school of Meier Graefe the German critic who devoted himself with exemplary ardour to defending the French Impressionists in Germany and Karl Scheffer "to learn" as he said "to become a good artist".

Meanwhile the first French paintings were beginning to appear in the Munich art galleries. In Bonnard, Klee admired "the economy of values" and the way in which the painter succeeded in restraining himself in order to bring out the bright tones. He rightly considered Vuillard weaker. Oddly enough he thought Vallotton was stronger. "But what an unpleasant painter", he hastens to add. Then there were two van Gogh exhibitions, which affected him profoundly. "At present," he notes in his Diary, "his pathos is foreign to me, but he is certainly a genius. Emotional to the point of being pathological. This is a brain which is suffering from the burning fire of a star. It frees itself through its works just before catastrophe overtakes it. A great tragedy is evolving in him, a tragedy of nature, a model tragedy." And he concludes: "I must be allowed to feel terror."

But it was in Cézanne, eight of whose pictures were exhibited by the 'Sezession', that he hailed a master rather than in van Gogh. Now he no longer hesitated to admit that the French interested him more than the Germans. From Berne, Ernst Sonderegger sent him as a present an etching by Ensor, *Skeletons trying to get warm*; this, too, was a decisive encounter for Klee. In 1908, he took the lease of a

SEVERITY OF THE CLOUDS. 1923. *Felix Klee Collection, Berne.*

CAMP ROAD. 1923. *Galerie Rosengart, Lucerne.*

little studio where he could paint in peace. It was in this studio that in 1910 he produced the well-known work in the Expressionist manner, *Girl with Jugs.* In Paris that same year Picasso painted the Cubist portrait of Vollard; he already had behind him all the Rose and Blue periods, which alone would justify his fame as a great artist. But Klee was one day to make up for the long wait.

Meanwhile Klee having discovered that a picture, like the human body, consisted of a skeleton, muscles and skin—that is to say that a picture had a special anatomy—stated that he in-

57

tended to paint: (*a*) space and (*b*) figures. He preferred the palette-knife to the brush, as being cleaner. Another of his methods of painting in oils was to spread the colour in flat washes on the canvas and to model them in order to obtain his light and shades.

He was taken up not only with colour but with line, which was to have such importance in his work. The line does not exist in nature. One can give an impression of nature by patches of colour and tones, he thought, for he was enthralled by the line of van Gogh and Ensor. Now his study of nature, to which he had devoted so many years,

allowed him to renew his attempts at "psychic improvisations". Without entirely losing sight of nature, he now wished to express the feelings which occupied his mind and heart and those events which can be translated into line even at the depth of night. He was undoubtedly right in thinking that only thus would his personality be "able to find fullest liberty".

It was in this state of mind that, in 1911, he began the illustrations to *Candide*, in which he suddenly rediscovered a childish freedom. Naturally his childishness had been long pondered, as he hastens to demon-

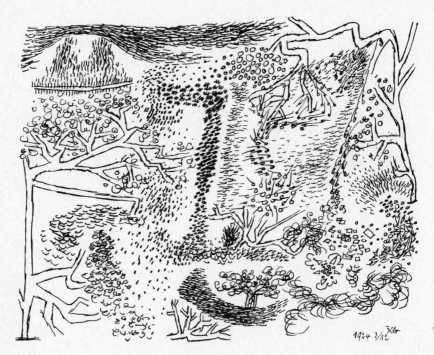

BLOSSOM. 1924. *Klee-Stiftung, Berne.*

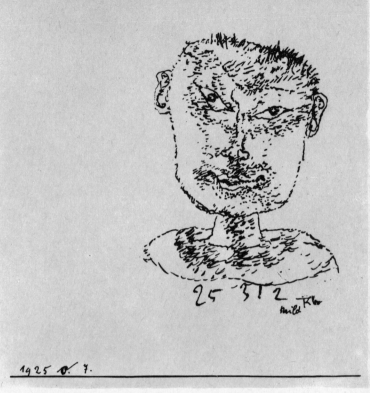

1925 o. 7.

SKETCH FOR A PORTRAIT. 1925. *Klee-Stiftung, Berne.*

strate with weighty arguments. Admittedly Carola Giedion-Welcker, with a woman's natural inquisitiveness, has discovered certain drawings by a mid-nineteenth-century illustrator, Martin Disteli, whom Klee cannot but have seen. But we prefer our own explanation to this learned discovery—namely that the characters in *Candide* and their poses are those which Paul Klee drew in early childhood with the coloured pencils his grandmother had given him as a present.

There is a greater freedom, too, in his other drawings, which are generally landscapes. Sometimes his line is still hard and loses itself in confused convolutions. But the adventure with the line has begun. The thoughtful self-portrait of 1911, however, is a considered and cordial act of homage to the technique of van Gogh.

NEAR TAORMINA (SIROCCO). 1924. Klee-Stiftung, Berne.

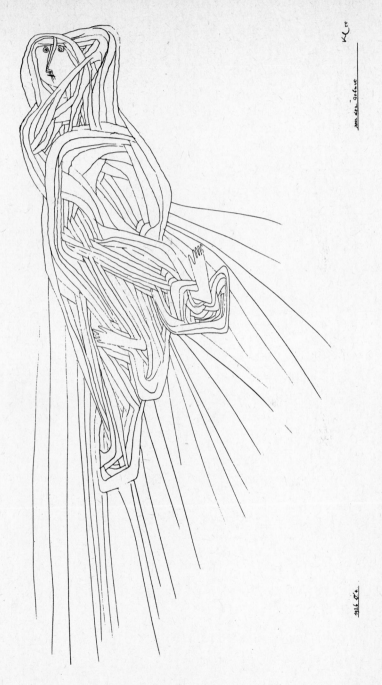

PREGNANT WOMAN. 1926. Klee-Stiftung, Berne.

61

NEIGHBOURLY IDYLL. 1926. *F. C. Schang Collection, New York.*

An exhibition in Switzerland in 1910 which went to Berne, Zürich, Basle and Winterthur—consisting of "56 well-framed sheets" did not pass unobserved. At Zürich one of his watercolours was bought for 200 marks. In Berne, Frau Hanni Bürgi decided to start a collection of his works. Summoning up his courage, Klee wrote to Lily, who had remained in Munich and who evidently ruled him with a rod of iron—even if she had the affection and the anxieties of a good wife—telling her that he could no longer do housework all day long and asking her to let him have half a day free for his work. He was now thirty; she was thirty-three.

But although the Exhibition had been well received in Berne and Zürich, it ended unfortunately; in Winterthur the public protested and the Museum, wishing to avoid trouble with the authorities, hastened to send back his works.

Fortunately he was no longer alone. A little circle of friends had formed round him. Above all there were his childhood friends—Bloesch and the Swiss painters, Kreydolf and Welti. The Zürich painter, Thomann, invited him to join the association known as 'Walze'. Thanks to Louis Moilliet he once more met Augustus Macke; Macke knew Kandinsky, who lived

FIGHT WITH THE DRAGON. 1926. *F. C. Schang Collection, New York.*

close to Klee. Louis Moilliet, who Klee often visited, also knew Kandinsky and went to and fro between them, showing them each other's work. After Kandinsky, whom Klee met personally in the autumn of 1911, other new friends came to comfort him for his set-backs—Franz Marc, who was to be his favourite of all, Campendonc, Jawlensky, Marianne von Werefkin and Gabrielle Münter. All these artists were to form a group which would make itself known to the public in Munich that same year under the name of 'Der Blaue Reiter'—the Blue Horseman.

Kandinsky was to have great in-fluence on his young colleague. Klee was ripe for this important new friendship for he had already written in his Diary: "More important than nature and its study is the ability to concentrate on the contents of one's own box of colours. I ought to be able to make free fantasies on the plane of colour." In the same way his study of light prepared him for the no less important meeting, it took place in Paris a few months later, in April 1912—with Robert Delaunay.

Klee found Kandinsky's works "bizarre". But after getting to know him personally he had great faith in the Russian artist who "is somebody and

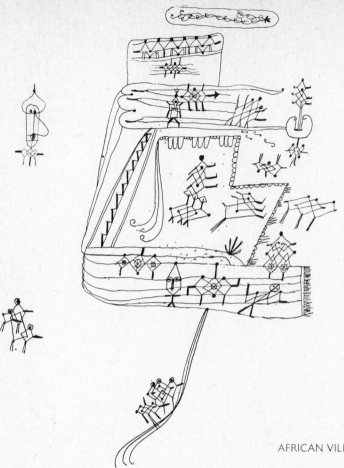

AFRICAN VILLAGE SCENE. 1925.

has a tremendously nice head''. Writing in a Swiss paper on the first 'Blaue Reiter' exhibition by Thannhauser, Klee said: "Kandinsky is the most audacious of them all, because he tries to convince us with words as well.'' He himself was invited to contribute to the second exhibition—it was limited to engravings—which was held in March 1912.

At this point Klee had no suspicion of the influence Kandinsky would have on him both through his work and through his writings, particularly his book, *Concerning the Spiritual Element in Art*. Although he admired Kandinsky he preferred Franz Marc—for one thing because Kandinsky was much older and he was slightly afraid of him. And yet he was to go a long way with Kandinsky.

CHILD ON THE STEPS. 1923. *Private Collection, Berne.*

HEAD OVER HEAD. 1926. *F. C. Schang Collection, New York.*

66

THE GREAT DOME. 1927. *Klee-Stiftung, Berne.*

Paris and Cubism

Klee's second visit to Paris would not have the importance which the critics rightly attribute to it had he not spent three hours out of that memorable fortnight with Robert Delaunay and the Cubists. These three hours enabled him to gain years by freeing him from the doubts which tormented him and by aiding him to find himself. Leaving little Felix with his grandparents in

Berne, Klee arrived in Paris on 2nd April 1912. That same evening his wife arrived from Munich to join him.

Their first week was given over entirely to sight-seeing. Lily wanted to satisfy her curiosity which, to be honest, was essentially that of a tourist. They saw the boulevards, the Seine, Notre-Dame, l'Opéra, Montmartre, the Sacré-Cœur, the Quartier Latin the Sainte-Chapelle and so on. In the evenings, except for one given over to

MATERIALISED GHOSTS. 1923. *Siegfried Rosengart Collection, Lucerne.*

THE BIRD CALLED PEP. 1925. *Private Collection, Berne.*

the Opéra—*Rigoletto* and ballet—they preferred popular amusements: the Bal Tabarin, the Moulin de la Galette and the Bal Bullier. Naturally they paid long visits to the Louvre, the Luxembourg and the Salon des Indépendants.

It was not until the morning of the 11th that he went to see Robert Delaunay in his studio. Sonia Delaunay, the painter's widow, has no recollec-

tion of the visit. No day went by without some unknown painter coming to see her husband, and Klee in these days was a young unknown painter.

Of that visit, which was to influence him so greatly, Klee merely wrote in his Diary: "Visited Delaunay in the morning in his studio." He says nothing of the pictures which Delaunay certainly showed him, nor of their conversation—perhaps because at this

AN INSIGNIFICANT FELLOW BUT OUT OF
THE ORDINARY . 1927.

Galerie Rosengart, Lucerne.

period he found it impossible to concentrate. Lily never left him for a
moment. In the evening they came
back late and tired. And on the evening
of the visit to Delaunay Lily wished to
go to the Bal Bullier, of which Klee had
spoken so much.

Next day Klee and his wife, together

with his friends Haller and Sonderegger, whom he had met in Paris, visited
the critic and dealer Wilhelm Uhde,
who had already shown his own
collection in Munich and was now
collecting the works of Rousseau,
Picasso and Braque while waiting for
"la peinture naïve" to which he would
eventually dedicate himself entirely.
In the house of another German dealer,
David Henri Kahnweiler, Klee saw
more Cubist paintings and works by
Derain and Vlaminck. On the 15th they
visited the flat of the Impressionists'
dealer, Durand-Ruel, who once a week,
like a Roman prince, allowed the
public to penetrate the privacy of his
house. On the same day, Lily left for
Munich after watching her husband
sign one hundred lithographs. That is
what the Diary says without giving any
other clue to the lithographs, of which
even the most painstaking of Klee's
biographers seem to be ignorant. Klee,
however, then left for Berne to collect
Felix and take him home.

The most important meeting during the visit was that with Robert
Delaunay. In the famous passage on
Fenêtres by Delaunay, Klee describes
him as "one of the most intelligent
artists of his time". He is much less
enthusiastic about Cubism. "Cubism,"
he writes in the same passage, "that
school of philosophers of form, has
found admirers in the field of landscape, but in the field of portraiture it
inevitably reveals its ridiculous nature.
Landscape can more easily suffer the
proportion of the objects represented
to be changed by simplification . . . the
result is always a landscape. Animals

BOTANICAL GARDEN. 1926. *Klee-Stiftung, Berne.*

SHIP Ꮒ C IN HARBOUR. 1925. *Private Collection, Berne.*

and men, which are created to live, lose something of their power to live with each deformation. Even when they have to be fitted into a heterogeneous plastic organism or, as with Picasso, broken up into separate patterns, they are assigned the place which the idea behind the picture demands." But, according to Klee, Delaunay avoids falling into these incongruities, by creating a type of independent picture, which has a totally abstract formal life "without motifs taken from nature".

None of this, of course, is very accurate. What Klee admired in Delaunay and would later admire in the Italian Futurists was movement; what he condemned in Cubism was its static quality. Thus we read in the Diary: "It is said that Ingres demanded repose, but I should like to demand—over and above feeling—movement." He must have translated with joy the article which Delaunay sent him some time later for *Der Sturm*, one of the first reviews dedicated to the new art in Europe. There Delaunay says: "Impressionism is the birth of light in painting. Light comes to us through our sensibility. Without visual sensibility there can be no light, no movement. Light creates in nature the movement of colours. Movement arises from the relationship between the disparate proportions of the contrasting colours themselves which constitute Reality. That reality has depth (we can see as far as the stars) and so becomes *simultaneity*. Simultaneity in terms of light is *harmony*, the rhythm of colours which creates man's vision. Human vision is endowed with the greatest

73

reality of all, since it comes to us directly from contemplation of the Universe. The eye is our most noble sense—the one which communicates most closely with our brain. Consciousness and the idea of the living movement of the world is *simultaneity*.''

THE MENAGERIE PARADES. 1926.
Private Collection, Berne.

These were ideas which Klee had been turning over for a long time. In 1910 he had written in his Diary: ''There is nothing new in producing light by heightening tones. Light as the movement of colours is something much newer.'' In short the two artists spoke the same language and had the same problems. Delaunay was well known in Germany. With his *Saint-Séverin* he had daringly posed the problem of space and perspective and influenced young De Chirico who, like Klee, studied painting in Munich. Theirs was a language for poets, musi-cians and painters. Klee, who was drawn now to nature, now to abstraction, but who could not completely detach himself from nature, found in Delaunay, the heir of post-Impressionism, a guide and model. On the other hand, Kandinsky, who at that period at least took his colours from nature, pushed Klee towards abstraction.

Delaunay was to influence Klee even more than Kandinsky. In the painter of the *Tour Eiffel*, Klee was to find what Picasso found in Matisse. The two poles of modern art devoured their contemporaries so to speak: the one,

74

BIRD DRAMA. 1920.
The Solomon Guggenheim Museum, New York.

uncle's restaurant, Klee had drawn his comments on the poems of Christian Morgenstern. Contrary to the opinion of the critics, who considered these drawings childish, there is already in the *Exciting Animals* of 1912 the Klee of 1925, with a line which is bold even

gently and almost as if he were begging their pardon; the other, brutally and almost joyfully.

Another happy encounter for Klee in 1913, was that with Arp. Arp, who was then twenty-five, had arranged an exhibition of *avant-garde* art in Zürich along with some friends. Klee welcomed the unknown young man courteously and showed him his drawings, among them those for *Candide*. After the illustrations to *Candide*, which recall both his first childish drawings and the arabesques he had admired as a boy in the veined marble table-tops in his

when it is forced into geometric patterns. The latter drawings dating from 1913, such as the *Policeman in Flight*, are less important and in the nature of puerile cartoons. The illustrations to *Candide* excited Arp greatly, and he promised to suggest to a friend of his—another Alsatian, Otto Flake, that they should be published. Flake had a great deal of influence with the publishers of the *Weissen Bücher*. Klee was greatly moved and, taking his violin from its case, began to play. Then he sat down beside his guest and asked for his news; as he listened he

SEMITIC BEAUTY. 1927. *Klee-Stiftung, Berne.*

CARNIVAL IN THE MOUNTAINS. 1924. *Klee-Stiftung, Berne.*

stroked a cat which lay curled up on his knees. At one point, Arp related recently, he noticed that Klee was removing fleas from the beast with extremely deft fingers and squashing them against the corner of the table with a sharp flick of his nail.

Some time later Klee visited Arp's exhibition and wrote an article on it for a review. Then he returned Arp's visit. He found him living in the utmost solitude near Weggis with his father,

who had left Alsace and set up a small factory in Switzerland in order not to see his sons in German uniform. But even the Arps' solitude was comforted by numerous friendships and Klee was welcomed "like a great man".

Arp is convinced that he succeeded in having the German translation of *Candide* with Klee's illustrations published in the *Weissen Bücher.* But the artist's bibliography contradicts this statement; it gives the first publication of *Candide* as 1920 in Munich under the editorship of Kurt Wolff.

Unlike Cubism, Italian Futurism aroused Klee's immediate sympathy; he considered Boccioni and Severini to be "very good" and went so far as to hail Carrà as the heir of Tintoretto and Delacroix. Yet in Klee's work it is easier to trace the influence of the Cubists than of the Futurists. If anything, it was in Carrà's metaphysical and not his Futuristic style and, above all, in De Chirico's first period, that Klee found fruitful models. His first impulses were never the most genuine. In this, too, he is the opposite of Picasso, who exists almost entirely on *coups de foudre*.

Finally, the year 1913 is extremely important for a number of works which reveal Klee's maturity—landscapes like the very beautiful *In the Quarry* (page 9), and pictures like that brilliant scene with its flavour of Cézanne, *Game of Cards in the Garden*.

These water-colours together with the charming *Young Woman in the green Blouse*—from Felix Klee's collection—are worthy of a great artist and it is strange that the critics have so far overlooked them.

Piper, the publisher, gave Klee further cause for satisfaction by inviting him to collaborate in a publication on the Expressionists. Herwarth Walden, the editor of *Der Sturm*, expressed the wish to exhibit some of his works in Berlin along with those of Franz Marc and Kubin—an artist whose principal merit is perhaps to have been one of the first admirers and collectors of Klee. Klee sent twenty-two pictures. It was his most important contribution to an exhibition since his one-man show in Switzerland. But an even more important event—his journey to Tunisia—soon made him forget these early successes, however much he had desired them.

PORTO-FERRAIO—ELBA. 1927. *Phil Hart, U.S.A.*

ANIMALS AT FULL MOON. 1927. *F. C. Schang Collection, New York*

Africa

After fifteen years of study, of experience and of fruitful exchanges, Paul Klee—although greatly esteemed by a small circle of friends—was still not the painter or the poet whom we admire today.

The journey to Tunisia on the initiative of his painter-friend, Louis Moilliet —in 1916 the Basle Museum acquired one of his pictures, the first modern work to be hung in a Swiss museum— finally put him on his road.

Moilliet knew a Swiss doctor in Tunis who had once invited him over. He proposed that his friends, Klee and Macke, should accompany him. The expenses of the trip were met because a chemist in Berne had bought several of their pictures. On 5th April the three friends were in Marseilles. Klee was fascinated by the city and would willingly have stayed there. He felt intensely the poetry of the old harbours and the contrast between the old streets sleeping in the sun and the noisy animation of the port.

The next day they embarked on the *Carthagène*, a new steamer belonging to the French Line. Klee, who had taken the precaution of providing himself with pills against sea-sickness, stood the crossing very well and could give himself up to the magic of the colours "of the air and the water", which gave a foretaste of the great revelation he was to experience a few days later in Kairouan.

"My father", wrote Felix Klee, "always felt the call of the South very strongly." In Tunis, at Carthage and at Kairouan, Klee seems to have re-discovered something of himself ("My real country?" he asked himself.) He had the feeling that he was re-establishing his ties with that civilization which, by some distant admixture, had given him his deep Moorish eyes. For the moment, he forgets his high-sounding statements about line and simultaneous contrasts in order to paint water-colours in which form is almost an accident of colour. If he thought of anyone in those days it must have been of Cézanne, his true master. But his colours, even if pale, are thicker, the brush strokes broader—almost

BERIDE (AQUATIC TOWN). 1927. *Klee-Stiftung, Berne.*

LITTLE PICTURE OF DICE. 1925. *Urvater Collection, Brussels.*

DWARF WITH A ROSE. 1927.

Rosengart Collection, Lucerne.

Klee's poetry, which nothing would ever be able to suffocate—neither his irony nor the dramatic pessimism of his last years with its roots in illness—was born on Easter Sunday on the shores of the Mediterranean. The evening before he had painted Easter eggs for his host's children and hidden them in the garden. Some days previously he had encountered a funeral on the outskirts of Tunis. Six mules pulled the hearse on which the coffin had been hoisted, all gold and bright blue. Round the hearse women were lamenting loudly. On that warm Easter evening everything that had struck him in the last few days—the landscape, melancholy with palms, the colour of the air and the sea, the starry sky, the immense new moon, the sultry noon tide, the meeting with the blue and gold hearse, the eggs hidden in the green bushes—everything came to life again in his mind like a fairy-tale "still very far away, very far, and yet so, so clear": a magic tale worthy of *The Thousand and One Nights*. Klee felt it stir him profoundly and permanently: "More than one blond moonrise of the North will call me in a low voice, like the blurred image in a mirror. It will be my betrothed, my other self. But I myself am the rising moon of the South."

In short, that evening Klee discovered his true vein of poetry. It was as if something which was already there, but repressed and cramped, had suddenly been liberated, freeing his imagination, which, even when forced to conform to certain patterns imposed by his sense of discipline, would remain

bands of colour. The division of space into horizontal or vertical sections recalls Delaunay.

The pages in which he recorded his unforgettable fortnight's stay in Tunisia are full of happiness—a happiness which is above all physical—and of calm confidence in his own powers. Even when he measures the long road ahead he is not at all depressed. It is no longer his earlier, rather overweening, confidence proclaimed with loud fanfares. It is confidence which comes from the heart and which he has long pondered.

lively and keen. Thus all his atavisms were happily reconciled.

Some days later at Kairouan he said: "I am possessed by colour—I do not need to pursue it. I know that it will possess me for ever. This is the great moment; I and colour are one. I am a painter." In life, as in his art, poetic emotion inevitably precedes plastic expression.

The actual water-colours he brought back to Berne—*View of Saint-Germain* (Cat. 11), *Motif from Hammamet* (Cat. 13), *Before the Gates of Kairouan*—were almost insignificant compared to those he carried in his head. The moon, the full moon of the South or the disturbing crescent of the Mussulman, the Biblical star, the strange plants, the little cupolas which we shall come across in later years, the greens, the bright yellows, the tints of sand and parched earth, the feeling for the Arab buildings and the little flags, certain mysterious signs which are fragments of Arabic script, the carpet texture of some compositions are, as it were, reflections of an experience which nothing could obliterate. The little square Arab houses meanwhile inspired his most orthodox essays in Cubism. To obtain pardon for the liberty he had taken, he then painted a surprising *Homage to Picasso* (Cat. 14), a play of brown and grey rectangles and squares set in an oval.

But unlike most men from the West who suddenly discover the Orient, he did not abandon himself to an orgy of colour. We cannot expect from Klee streams of chromatic colour and apocalyptic blazes; instead we find that

ORIENTATED MAN. 1927.

Private Collection, U.S.A.

precise sense of colour, which comes from perfect tonal harmony, or the jewelled splendour of a single hue, of a simple patch of colour. He is above all one of those painters of 'feeling', of whom Bonnard said: "He produces a closed world, a picture which is in the nature of a book and carries its interest with it wherever it goes. One imagines this artist spending a great deal of time doing nothing but looking around and looking within."

Suddenly, on the eve of his departure,

SLIGHT DANGER AT SEA. 1928. *Klee-Stiftung, Berne.*

FULL MOON. 1927. *Private Collection, Berne.*

he felt the need to be alone, to eat alone in the best Italian restaurant in Tunis, to embark alone—third class —for Palermo, where he admired the "strong personality" of the mountain which dominates the city. In Naples and Rome he felt he had returned after only a few days' absence. Instead twelve years had passed since his first fruitful stay. He did not even stop in Florence. Milan was only a compulsory break in his journey as he waited for the train for Berne.

Admittedly he was short of money, but in his haste there was, above all, fear of losing by the way that treasure of images and sensations which he wished to bring home intact. Without that treasure, the war, which was about to break out would have been much more painful and perhaps even fatal to him.

CASTLE OF THE ORDER. 1929. *Klee-Stiftung, Berne.*

86

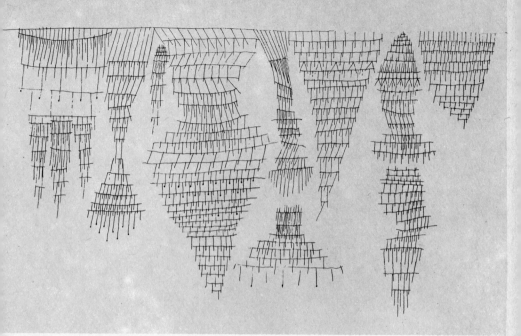

RAIN. 1927. *Klee-Stiftung, Berne.*

War

If it is true, as Carola Giedion-Welcker states, that immediately after the war "Klee seems to flourish like a tropical plant", it was during the war that he struck down roots and grew in stature. It was during the war that at last "everything became Klee". Soon after his return from Tunis and the outbreak of the war, of whose useless horrors he had had a presentiment as is demonstrated by some drawings dated 1913, poetry and painting fused into those ideograms which he called "picture-poems".

The war cut Klee off from the outside world and forced him to take refuge in himself. This, as he himself confesses, was the real source of abstraction as far as he was concerned. In a happy world there is a pleasure in looking around one; but in a world full of moral and material ruin the only comfort lies in memories of days lived intensely.

"Everything becomes Klee"—but in a dream, a sort of *rêve éveillé*, which leads the Surrealists to recognize in him one of their most authoritative precursors. Although he did not lose sight of new orientations, such as the example of Delaunay and the Cubists, movement, light, colour and space,

87

COAST OF PROVENCE. 1927. *F. C. Schang, New York.*

were thought out anew by Klee in essentially poetic terms.

It may seem surprising that a person of Klee's sensitivity could so easily dissociate himself from the anguish of the war and concentrate on his work. The death at the front, a few weeks after the outbreak of hostilities, of Macke, with whom he had the bond of the journey to Tunis, did not seem to move him excessively, or at least no more than the death in childbirth of the wife of his other travelling companion, Louis Moilliet. "I have carried this war within me for a long time", he confided to his Diary. "And that is why it no longer concerns me internally." It must not be forgotten that he was not a real German, moreover the fact that he had passed his childhood in Switzerland had no doubt taught him the futility of military adventures. However, as a German on the reserve, he did his duty but without zeal. Not having been called up, he was granted a passport by the military authorities to go to Switzerland, where he wanted to visit his family. He had to promise to come back to Germany at the end of his stay. "What would I be without Germany?" he protested sincerely.

All his friends were called up, like Franz Marc, or scattered, like Kandinsky, who had gone back to Russia, Jawlensky and Marianne von Werefkin, whom he found in Switzerland. The *Weissen Bücher* hesitated to publish *Candide* and, like most publishers when they cannot reach a decision, withdrew into hostile silence. Only one ray of light illuminated the gloomy scene—

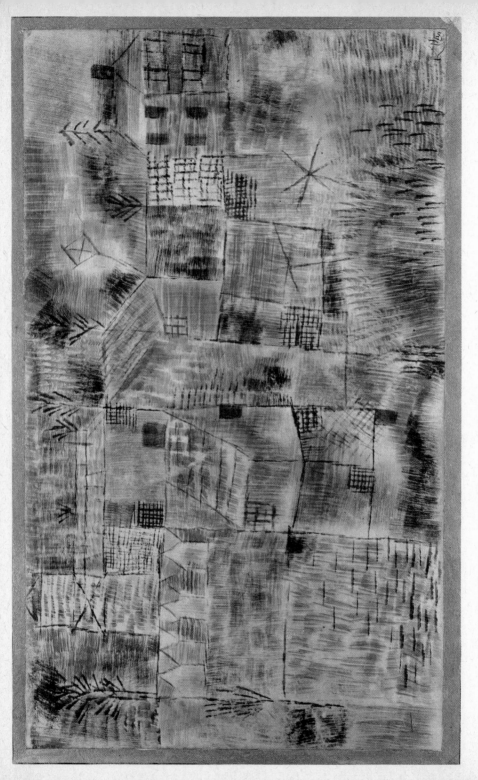

VILLAGE WITH RISING KITE. 1925. Angela Rosengart Collection, Lucerne.

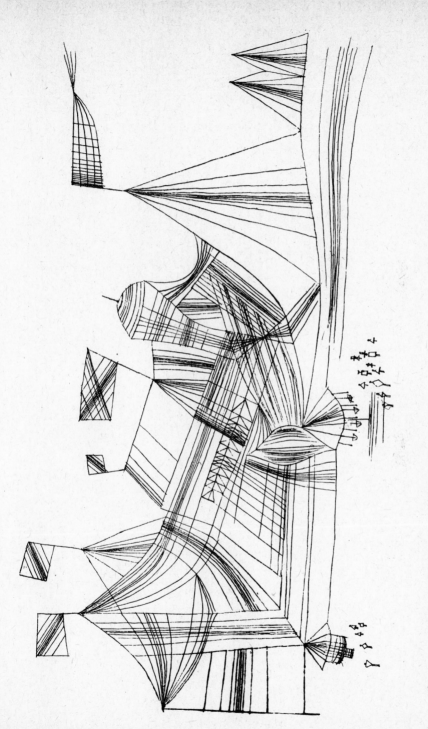

BIG CIRCUS. 1928. *Private Collection, Berne.*

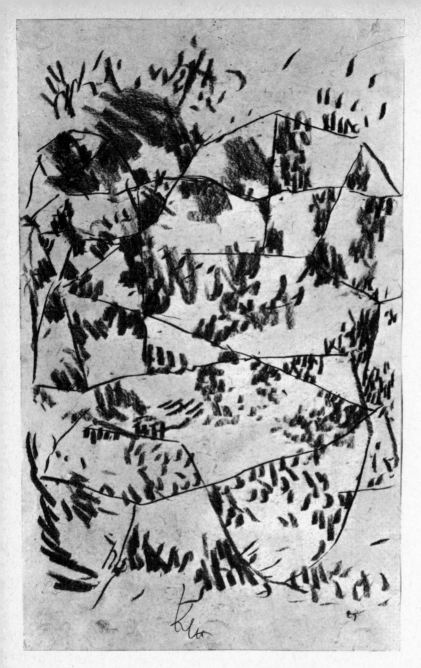

DESERT MOUNTAINS. 1929. *Klee-Stiftung, Berne.*

SONG TO THE MOON. 1927. *Klee Stiftung, Berne.*

the acquaintance with Rilke, who was already famous as the author of the *Stundenbuch*. Rilke admired Klee the draughtsman more than Klee the painter. They frequently met either in Klee's flat or in the vast studio shared by Rilke and his friend, Lou Albert-Lazar. Klee, to keep the talk off the war, organized small concerts with his wife and some friends. The poet's external "elegance" aroused the painter's amazement. "How does he do it?" he asked.

Speaking of this friendship, Jean Warmoes has recently stated that Klee brought Rilke sixty of his compositions in colour, which he left with the poet for several months so that he could study them at his leisure. Thus Rilke was at last able to form a clear idea of the transition from painting from nature to abstraction. In a letter to his friend, Lou Balladine, dated 23rd February 1921, he writes as follows:

"They attracted me and held my attention all the more because one could still feel the influence of Kairouan, which I know. . . . During these war years I have often had exactly the same feeling that reality was disappearing;

for it is a question of faith to know to what degree we accept reality and then attempt to express ourselves through it. Broken and mutilated creatures are best rendered by their own debris. What is astonishing—apart from the disappearance of the subject proper—is that at present music and graphic art take each other for subject. This short circuit in the arts, of which nature and even the imagination know nothing, is—as far as I am concerned—the most disturbing phenomenon of the present day; yet it is a phenomenon which liberates, since farther than that one cannot go."

Franz Marc came to visit him on his short leaves. Klee played Bach fugues for him; Marc, quite unimpressed by the splendour of the lieutenant's uniform he was wearing, listened to him and turned over the pages of Jawlensky's *Variations*.

In March 1916 Klee too was called to the colours. At almost the same time he had a telegram with the news of the death at Verdun of Franz Marc, his dearest friend—a man of whom he could not think without, as a reflex, thinking of himself, so much did they have in common, even if Klee felt himself to belong to a different sector of artistic creation.

Military life for a soldier in the German territorial forces was not unbearable. The long marches distracted Klee, who did not feel the least cast down at regularly confusing the targets on the ranges. Otherwise his attitude was that the war must not prevent him from painting and taking part in exhibitions. He worked unknown to his superiors, converting a box into his workshop. He painted with the paper on his knees under the table. Then he was transferred to Gersthofen where, having almost nothing to do, he found time to read Chinese poetry and collections of children's verses. He was given a short

WAVES. 1929. *Felix Klee Collection, Berne.*

THE RENDEZVOUS. 1929. *F. C. Schang Collection, New York.*

leave to be present at the *vernissage* of an exhibition of his work in Berlin arranged by the periodical *Der Sturm*. His works began to sell and he himself both to reap the first-fruits of his work and to read the first critiques of his work. But the most welcome reward was the financial one. Now he was sure that, when he returned to Munich on demobilization, he could engage a maid. A big Leipzig weekly asked him for a photograph of a picture for reproduction. He hastened to enquire how much he would get for the reproduction

rights. But this was not mere greed on his part. One of his favourite pastimes was book-keeping—a pastime he could pursue even in his regiment for they made him look after the regimental funds, after keeping him in a workshop painting aeroplane wings. At the end of the war he possessed a considerable sum thanks to the payments made by his dealers, Walden and Goltz, for the sale of his pictures.

Even among the greatest there are very few artists who, like Klee, have had the good fortune to see their first

95

LITTLE PORTRAIT OF GIRL IN YELLOW. 1925. *F. C. Schang Collection, New York.*

artistic successes crowned with financial success. But undoubtedly Klee's water-colours, in spite of some easily identifiable influences, reveal a new and powerful artistic personality. He was confirmed in his conviction that true painting can only be painting of the feelings. Looking out of the window one day at dusk, he thought that the diffused light of a slight haze can be richer in colour than a sunny day; but

CHILD AND DOG. 1929. *Collection of Mrs. Robert Cage, Milford, Conn.*

he considered it folly to attempt to fix it on canvas as the Impressionists would have done; the moment of time is too short. One must give the mind time to be penetrated by the event. And this, French painting from Delacroix on seems to have forgotten.

It was Klee's great merit to realize at once that Braque's 'inventions', such as the insertion of letters or numbers in a picture, have no other scope than a poetic one. So too with the newspaper cuttings and the coloured paper in the 'papiers collés'. As he was taken by Braque's letters so he was by De Chirico's arrows, Delaunay's little crosses and windows, and the doors of the 'metaphysical' painters. All these elements mingled with the images of his own past and the memories of days of happiness. A "cosmic community" occupied his mind. He dreamt of

97

LONG HAIR SOULFUL. 1929. *F. C. Schang Collection, New York.*

moons and stars, arrows and suns. Certain signs—like the exclamation mark—forced themselves upon him because there is nothing corresponding to them in plastic art.

The subjects of his work—the 'themes' which have been so much discussed—he owed to either artistic

BARBARIC, CLASSICAL, SOLEMN. 1926. *Eric Estorick, London.*

memories, *Carpet of Memory* (Cat. 12) or to literature, *The Death of the Nightingale* (1917). At other times they arise from graphic or formal inventions like the astonishing *Ab ovo* (Cat. 21) or the *Little Vignette in Egypt* (page 21). Works like *Chamber architecture* or the *Anatomy of Aphrodite* (page 17) are pure abstractions, but even in his abstract works he is forced to rediscover those signs which drift through his mind and which, like the pine and the moon, have become his own symbols. In 1917 he even reduced the *Rainbow* to a pure abstract design, as in *Colour Corner* (Cat. 18) of the

same year he did the metaphysical labyrinths of De Chirico, realizing that painting cannot simply be Wilde's "symbols and space".

Sometimes in his creative fervour he felt the need to work contemporaneously on compositions which had nothing in common and which re-

FAMILY WALK. 1930. *Klee-Stiftung, Berne.*

quired different techniques. At other times he was possessed by the mania for variations. He knew that the spectator wishes to be astonished like Diaghilev saying to young Cocteau: "Étonne-moi." Klee accepted the challenge and no one will probably ever succeed in being the source of more astonishment than he.

In later years, stumbling on the memory of these first happy compositions, the initial drawings which he jealously preserved, Klee did not hesitate to reshape them, just as between

1915 and 1918 he rethought Cubism and, round about 1930, Neo-division-ism.

The question is whether these 're-thinkings' really brought him nearer to what he called the "heart of creation". Undoubtedly so, if the "heart of creation" is poetry, as in his work. But we must not see in him as Joseph-Emile Müller justly remarks, "a mere case of inspiration. He is not the irresponsible voice of something which shakes him and dominates him in spite of himself. He is at the same time

FEAR OF BECOMING DOUBLE. 1929.

Galerie Rosengart, Lucerne.

By mixing chalk and colours Klee did not propose to give the illusion of a fresco. Unlike the Cubists he replaced the reality of daily life, of the daily paper, by an ageless reality. He transferred the law of contrasts from the field of optics to that of metaphysics and drew the most extreme conclusions

a craftsman and this craftsman is very deliberate, very methodical. He knows the nature of all his materials, for part of his work has consisted precisely in examining them one after another in order to master them with intelligence.''

The complex alchemy of his water-colours, as of his oil-paintings, is due essentially to his previous researches and to the example of Cubism, which had proposed to use new materials, but had then repented of its own audacity and gone back to traditional materials.

from it. Dissatisfied with pure colour he mixed oils with tempera colours and water-colours: he scraped the paper or canvas even using a pumice-stone; he mixed glue and varnish. He is himself unsure whether to consider one of his paintings an oil-painting or a water-colour. He even calls certain of his drawings in Chinese ink, ink-water-colours if diluted with water; nor is he wrong, for even black is a colour— indeed, as Renoir said, the queen of colours. What he is most concerned with is the truth, the solidarity, the time-resisting quality of his colours. Nor is it true to say that his colour is always cramped. He is one of the rare colourists of our age.

He was a musician and did not claim to make his works the equivalent of a musical composition—merely a motif, a brief melodic phrase. In a picture space and time are not what they are in music. In Klee a musician will perhaps one day find much of Bach and Mozart, and in his later works, Hindemith and Schönberg.

If we take the works painted during the war and add the landscapes from the years 1919 to 1920, on them there is "all Klee". In *Rhythm of Autumn Trees* we find once more the horizontal bands of the 'ideograms' which allowed Klee to divide plastic space into musical measures as in the *Red and White Domes* (1914). With the

ideograms and the geometrical compositions like *Castle Garden* (1919) he looks forward to the 'magic squares' of the Weimar period. Klee the mystic of the tragic years is already present in the first symbolical compositions of 1918, *With the Eagle* (Cat. 24) and *The Descent of the Dove*, Klee the romantic in *Blue Roof and Orange Moon* and in *The Nightingale Singing*. There is above all the conflict between North and South, between fragile pines and fanatic moons —these almost indestructible symbols of his period of happiness. Living figures are rare but there is the disquieting *Canary Magician* painted in Munich in 1920. There are few studies directly from nature, which in 1913 had given us the splendid water-colour *In the Quarry* (page 9) and then all the Tunisian water-colours. The artist now seeks for his inspiration within himself.

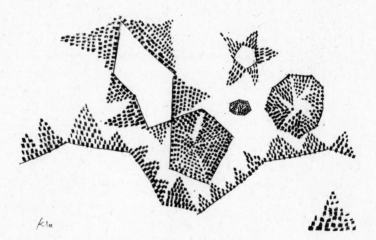

STUDY. 1931. *Klee-Stiftung, Berne.*

102

FLAGGED TOWN. 1927. *Private Collection, Berne.*

CONSTRUCTION BASED ON VARIATIONS. 1927. *Klee-Stiftung, Berne.*

'Creative Confession'

Klee's *Creative Confession* was published in a little collection appearing in 1920, which contains essays by a score of poets, playwrights, painters and musicians; among them Benn, Unruh, Toller, Pechstein, Beckmann, Marc and Schönberg. Klee had made an earlier version of his essay at the end of 1918 at Gersthofen, shortly before demobilization. According to Jurg Spiller, he at that time called these few pages, which the recent appearance of Kandinsky's *Painting considered as Pure Art* had greatly encouraged him to write, *Thoughts on Drawing and on Art in general.*

The essay—it is Klee's first publication—begins with a short sentence which summed up the reflections and experiences of twenty years of work; for the twenty years of hectic creation which followed, it would remain the formula which epitomized the essentials of his view of art. "Art does not reproduce the visible; it renders visible." But these reflections, as the original title indicated, flow from the experience of Klee the draughtsman. The nature of graphic art easily tempts one to abstraction and rightly so. The purer the draughtsmanship—that is to say, the more stress is laid on the formal elements which are the basis of the drawing—the more inadequate is the framework for the realistic representation of visual objects. But this formula once again reveals a truth arrived at by a long period of work. It is a conclusion, a result; the task was now to get back to the elements. "The

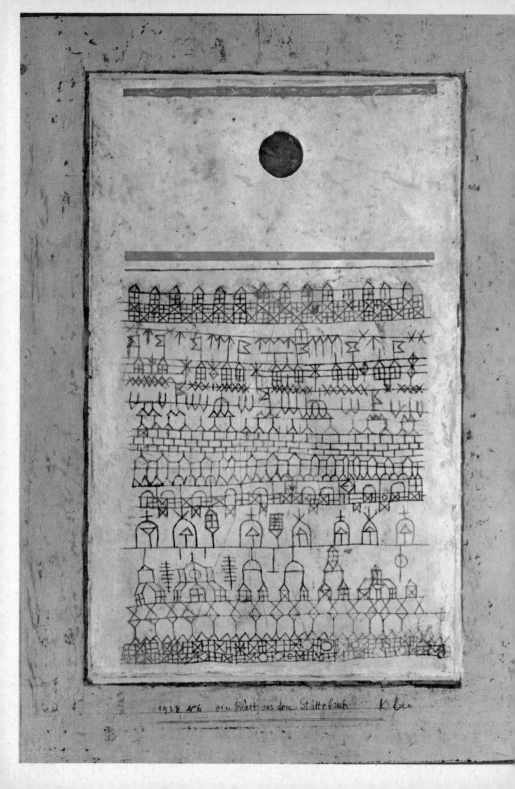

1928 N°6   ein Blatt aus dem Städtebuch   Klee

FEAR BEHIND THE CURTAIN. 1929. *Galerie Rosengart, Lucerne.*

formal elements of drawing are: points, the energy of the line, surface and space.'' The element of surface, for instance, will be the energy produced by means of a thick pencil. An example of the element of space is a cloudy, vaporous mark produced by a full brush with varying degrees of strength.

In order to multiply and vary his examples and make us see them in the most concrete manner possible, Klee proposes to his reader to accompany him on a walk, a little excursion into the country; we shall see how the phenomena of nature are represented by the graphic elements and their combinations. We start off from a point: that gives us a line. We stop once or twice; the line has been broken or articulated. We cross a river by boat— an undulatory movement. A ploughed field—a surface scored with lines. Mist

A LEAF FROM THE TOWN RECORDS. 1928.
Kunstmuseum, Basle.

in a valley—a spatial element. We meet people. Basketmakers coming home with their cart (a wheel). They have a child with them with funny curls (a corkscrew motion). Later the weather becomes sultry and lowering (spatial element). A flash of lightning on the horizon (a zigzag line). There are still stars overhead (scattered dots). The day comes to an end. We reach the inn and here Klee, who was certainly thinking of many such walks he had taken in the Swiss countryside or near Munich, concludes: "Before we fall asleep many things will recur to our memory, for a little journey like this is rich in impressions." To sum up he writes: "All kinds of different lines. Blobs of colour. Stippling. Stippled and striped surfaces. Undulatory movement. Broken, articulated movement. Counter-movement. Objects interlaced and interwoven. Masonry, peeling stone. Harmony with one voice. With several voices. Line losing itself, gaining strength (dynamic)."

Thus certain elements of graphic representation have been named and catalogued, but in order to constitute forms or objects, the combination of several elements will usually be necessary and it follows that "thanks to such enrichment of the symphony of forms, the possibilities of variation and, thereby, the possibilities of expression are multiplied to infinity"

Klee next examines the essential relationships between the work of art and time (or movement). "At the roots of the process of becoming there is always movement." He begins by discarding the traditional distinction

GIRL WITH DOLL. 1930.
Chris. Schang Collection, Westport, Conn.

between the spatial and temporal arts —a distinction formulated by Lessing in his *Laocoön*, in which Klee sees merely the invention of a pedant: "For space too is a temporal concept." The elements of graphic representation are engendered in time: "When a point becomes movement and a line, that demands time. Similarly, when a line shifts to produce a surface. So too with the movement from surfaces to space."

And the work of art? Its creation is subject to the same law. "It is constructed piece by piece, exactly like a house."

But the artist, when he reflects on the birth of a work, does not forget "the other man, the man who looks at the picture. Does he finish with the work in a single glance? Alas, yes, only too often." But anyone seriously interested in painting requires time and that was why Feuerbach said that to understand a picture you need a chair. "So that the wearying legs will not disturb the mind." Thus everywhere there is time and movement; that is the universal law. "The genesis of script is an excellent example of movement. The work of art is also first and foremost, genesis. A fiery desire for realization flashes from the artist's brain; passes through his hand, spreads over the canvas, then, completing the circle, returns like a spark to his eye and mind. The eye, like the artist, comes and goes, works and rests." The essential work of the man who looks at pictures is also temporal. Klee sums up his concept with these words: "Plastic art was born of movement, is itself movement caught and held and is registered in movement (eye muscles)."

But the artist of today no longer sees things as they were seen yesterday. "People used to reproduce things seen

ANIMAL HAVING A WALK. 1930. *Angela Rosengart Collection, Lucerne.*

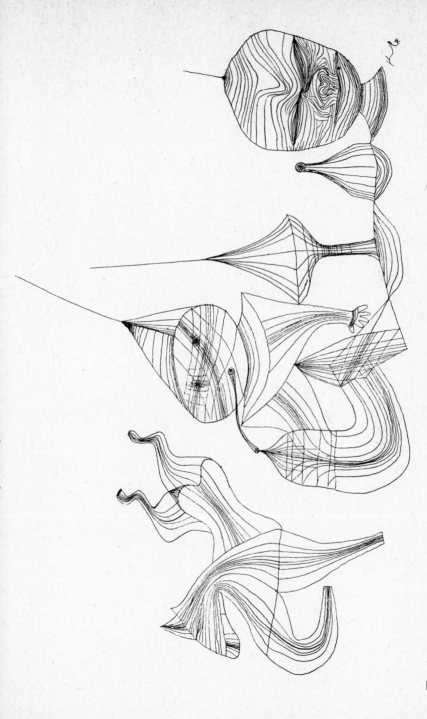

OVERTONES. 1928. *Private Collection, Berne.*

on earth—things which had been or would be seen with pleasure. Today the reality of visible objects has been revealed and the belief has been expressed that, in relation to the universe, the visible is only an isolated case and that other truths exist latently and are in the majority."

Just as the simultaneous existence of the male and female principles constitute ethical stability, so in the domain of the plastic arts there is a corresponding "simultaneous combination of forms, movement and counter-movement or—to put it more naïvely—contrasting objects (chromatically: the use of fragmented colour-contrasts, as in Delaunay)". In the work of art every force requires a complementary power to attain a state of equilibrium.

Klee has taken us a long way on the path towards abstraction and generalization. Coming back to earth he gives some concrete examples. To the

SPECIAL DOOR. 1932. *Klee-Stiftung, Berne.*

TOWN WITH WATCHTOWERS. 1929. *Klee-Stiftung, Berne.*

OLD TOWN AND BRIDGE. 1928. *R. Doetsch-Benziger Collection, Basle.*

experiences of a sailor of long ago in his little boat there corresponded the vision of ancient man; modern man on the other hand, walking the deck of a ship is familiar with his own movement, that of the boat, the direction and speed of the current, the rotation of the earth, the course of the stars. "Result: an agglomeration of movements in the universe with as its centre myself and the steamer." Another example: an apple-tree in blossom—an agglomeration of various stages of growth. Third example: a man asleep —an agglomeration of functions united in repose.

In these lines Klee reveals his secret to us—the mechanism of the image. The apple-tree in blossom lives and grows before our eyes—here are "its roots, the mounting sap, its trunk, a cross-section of the trunk to show the thickness of the wood, the flower and its structure, its sexual functions, the fruit, core and seeds".

All the operations which he describes

114

and which are associated in artistic creation—that is to say, the liberation of the elements and their regrouping, the dismembering and reconstruction of the whole, 'plastic polyphony', the conquest of repose by the equilibrium of movements—all these are of decisive importance for understanding the construction of forms. "But that is not art in its most exalted form. In its most exalted form there is behind the ambiguity a last mystery and at that point the light of the intellect dies away miserably." It is thanks to this element of mystery that art can have such a powerful effect on us, that our imagination can remind us of experiences which cheer and excite us more than any conscious terrestrial or super-terrestrial states, and that "symbols comfort the spirit". Klee ends with an enthusiastic and joyful appeal, with an invitation to enjoy the possibility which art offers us "of having a change of point of view just as we have a change of air".

AN HABITUE. 1931. *Klee-Stiftung, Berne.*

The Bauhaus

Thus in 1920, when Gropius asked him to come to the Bauhaus in Weimar, Klee had already written his *Creative Confession*, which was being printed by Reiss of Berlin.

In the Bauhaus, Walter Gropius proposed to create a new corporation of artists and artisans. Abolishing all barriers between themselves they were to collaborate in the construction of a new order which was both artistic and ethical. Architecture, sculpture and painting were to form a harmonious unity.

Gropius succeeded in immediately surrounding himself with collaborators worthy of the task—Feininger and Oskar Schlemmer, Moholy-Nagy and George Muche, the sculptor Gerhard Marcks and the architect Meyer. Paul Klee joined them in January 1920, deserting his beloved Munich. Two years later, Kandinsky arrived from Moscow with his young wife.

The Bauhaus was certainly unlike any other school. It aimed, as we have seen, to rediscover the harmony between the various departments of art—above all between the strictly artistic activities and the handicrafts.

RICH LAND. 1931. *Felix Klee Collection, Berne.*

RESONANCE OF THE SOUTHERN FLORA. 1927.

The traditional division between the fine and applied arts was ignored. "Our final aim, although it is still distant", said the inaugural manifesto, "is the unitary work of art, the Great Work, which will do away with all distinctions between monumental and decorative art."

In reality, the Bauhaus was an advanced school of form and as such left its mark on a period of extremely fruitful experiment; round about 1925 it evolved a style which was everywhere much admired and which bears its name. There is no doubt that the Bauhaus contributed greatly to the evolution of both Klee's and Kandinsky's thought, to the formation of their personal theories and to their particular dialectic. However there is no such break between Munich and Weimar in Klee's work as Cubism produced in the work of Picasso.

A short essay published by Klee in a collection produced by the Bauhaus in 1923 is extremely useful for understanding his art. In it—the title is *Wege des Naturstudiums* (Approaches to the study of Nature)—we once more find the intimate tone of the *Creative Confession*.

"For the artist the dialogue with nature remains a *sine qua non*. The artist is a man, himself nature and a part of nature, within nature's space." This axiom expresses a general and constant truth; what vary from time to time are the methods of studying nature, which is a necessary condition of artistic creation. But one must not let oneself be misled as to the real importance of such innovations. "The methods seem very new without perhaps really being so." On this point Klee's judgment shows every sign of being seriously weighed: we must not minimize the joy we experience from the discovery of new roads, but on the other hand the artist's knowledge of the past must prevent him from "frantically seeking novelty at the expense of the natural".

What characterizes the art of yesterday in its relationship to the natural world is that it is a study, a "laboriously detailed examination of appearances". "The 'I' and the 'you', the artist and his subject, attempted to establish relationship by the optico-physical path through the layer of air which lies between the 'I' and the 'you'." The positive aspect of this method is that it has given us "excellent pictures of the surface of objects", the negative aspect of things. "The art of contemplation, the art of revealing non-optical impressions and images was neglected." One must, therefore, without underestimating the advances made by increased knowledge of phenomena, carry it further. "The artist of today is more than an official photographer trained to the pitch of perfection; he is more complicated,

MORE AND MORE SIGNS. 1932. *Klee-Stiftung, Berne.*

119

CHURCH AND CASTLE. 1929. *Felix Klee Collection, Berne.*

more rich and greater in stature. He is a creature living on the earth, a creature living at the centre of the universe—that is to say a creature on a star among other stars.''

Our knowledge of the individual object grows in scope and depth and does not stop at appearances. We know that there is more to it than the external aspect. Man dissects the object and as he cuts it open reveals its interior. "Experiences of this kind, duly added together, permit the 'I'

to deduce the interior of the object from its exterior; this it does intuitively in so far as the 'I' is encouraged by optico-physical means to draw from the exterior conclusions of an affective nature which can intensify the impression of the phenomenon to the point of functional interiorization.''

But there are other lines of approach which lead to a 'humanization' of the subject and bring the 'I' and the subject into a relationship which goes beyond optical foundations. "First of

OLD MAN CALCULATING. 1929.

all there is the non-optical approach of our common roots in the earth, which reaches the eye from below, and secondly, the non-optical approach of the cosmic community, which reaches us from above. If this type of study is repeated and intensive it leads to a genuine experience."

Klee adds that the lower approach runs through the static zone and produces static forms, while the upper approach runs through the dynamic zone. This is a somewhat obscure concept but he elaborates it as follows: "On the lower approach, which has its centre of gravity at the centre of the earth, lie all the static problems which might be defined in the words: 'Stand up in spite of all the chances of falling.' One is led to the upper paths by one's aspirations to liberate oneself, by swimming or flight, from the bonds of the earth and so to attain full liberty, liberty through movement.

"All these paths meet in the eye and from that point, being translated into form, lead to a synthesis of external vision and internal contemplation. . . .

"Through experiences acquired in these different ways—experiences which he has transformed into creative work—the artist gives proof of the degree of intimacy of his 'dialogue with nature'.

"The further he progresses with his vision of nature and with meditation, the freer he is to organize groups of abstract forms, which go beyond the schematic and the arbitrary and achieve a new natural order, the natural order of the work of art. Then he creates a work or he participates in the creation of works which are images of the handiwork of God".

In the *Pädagogisches Skizzenbuch* (Pedagogical sketches), which appeared in 1924, Klee addresses himself more to his pupils. It is a little scholastic manual, which does not interest us particularly in this context. Klee was undoubtedly a good teacher. But it is doubtful whether all his pupils were capable of understanding his doctrine. In the special number which the Swiss periodical *Du* devoted to Klee in October 1948, one of his ex-pupils admits that "Klee's extraordinary knowledge of form, of the techniques

CLOISONNE. 1928. *Siegfried Rosengart Collection, Lucerne.*

GENESIS OF THE PHYSIOGNOMY. 1929. *Felix Klee Collection, Berne.*

of drawing and colour and of their possibilities, had allowed him in a very short time to communicate to his pupils that power of the symbol which is unconsciously present in children and which in Klee was accurately controlled—a system which has occupied creative artists ever since. However . . . the most subtle and most subtly imagined formal elements, which in Klee's case were certainly products of his own mind, led his pupils to hollow, untidy imitations, . . . Klee can scarcely have avoided seeing this. But he did not wish to admit that it happened with his pupils. Although ordinarily a tolerant man, on this point he was impatient and even angry. Excellent teacher though he was in his own field, Klee had little capacity for *educating* others. He completely lacked the Socratic touch; indeed he hated it. His pupils' work seems ageless, like his own creations. The true educator, on the other hand, protects the germinating seed and brings it to maturity; but in the case of Klee's pupils the first shoots were already harvested to form the actual material for their pictures. His pupils had come to know their 'original state' but they lacked the long-studied ability,

FLIGHT FROM ONESELF. 1931. *Klee-Stiftung, Berne.*

124

DOWNWARDS. 1932. *Private collection, U.S.A.*

amounting almost to scientific objectivity, which their master possessed and which enabled him to pass from intuition to knowledge. . . . The pupils could extract material from the depths of their subconscious or unconscious, but they lacked the ability to connect it with reality—an ability which Klee possessed in its purest form. For Klee was not only a great innovator who strove to see behind things, he was also an exceptionally gifted observer and realist.

"Another of his powers—it allowed him to use the means of plastic expression as the actual content of a painting —Klee could only put at his pupils' disposal to a very limited degree. Here his starting-point was a knowledge of graphology; he gave to his written or painted symbols new and original overtones. In so doing he never lapsed into producing anything indefinite or ill-defined, because the execution of his compositions was subject to his own nature and to his own laws, which were not however transmissible. So his pupils went astray and lost their necessary link with the world around them. . . ."

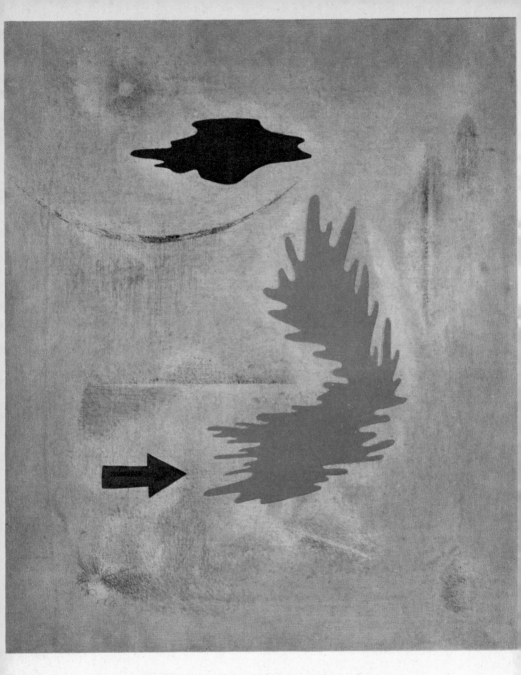

MIXED WEATHER. 1929. *Felix Klee Collection, Berne.*

GROUP INTERLACED. 1930. *Klee-Stiftung, Berne.*

Line, Tonality, Colour

"Pictures look at us", said Klee in a famous lecture given at Jena in January 1928 on the occasion of an exhibition of his works. The theorist in him had a powerful antagonist—the mystic. To reconcile them, to unite them in a common effort, was until his death his most constant endeavour.

The Jena lecture is his 'discourse of method'. In it, like Kandinsky, he deals with the most abstract aspects of the problems of creation. When it was published in 1945, under the title *On Modern Art*, it aroused deep interest.

Klee begins by explaining that he would have preferred to deal principally with those parts of the creative process which take place in the unconscious; but to do so would be to forget that the majority of his hearers were more familiar with the content of a work of art than with its formal aspect. He would therefore discuss questions of form. "I am going" he said "to give you a glimpse into the painter's workshop."

There must be some ground common to both artists and public where they can meet and the artist cease to appear to them as a strange phenomenon. In fact, the artist is a being who, like everyone else, has been

BETWEEN AUTUMN AND WINTER. 1932. *Klee-Stiftung, Berne.*

ATTACK BY THOSE COMING AFTER. 1933. *Curt Valentin Collection, New York.*

placed in a complex world without being consulted, and like everyone else, he must get along in it as best he can. He differs from other people only in this that he solves his problems with his own special methods and that by so doing he is sometimes, perhaps, happier than the non-creative person, who never succeeds in performing a truly creative, liberating action.

"Let us take an artist" he goes on, "who is sufficiently well 'orientated' in the world and in life to be able to arrange in an orderly way phenomena and experiences. I should like to compare this orientation among the things of the natural world and of life, this complex order, to the multiple ramifications of the roots of a tree". The sap, coming from below, penetrates into the artist and reaches his eye. He is like the trunk of the tree. Under the pressure and urgency of this powerful upsurge he transmits what he has seen into his work; his work, like the crown of the tree, expands and is visible in time and space. No one would ever think of demanding that a tree should grow a crown exactly like its root. Different functions assume different forms. But people would like to forbid the artist to depart from his model; if he does so, he is accused of incompetence

129

TABLE OF COLOUR (IN GREY MAJOR). 1930 *Klee-Stiftung, Berne.*

or of deliberate falsification. But like the tree, he is merely collecting and transmitting forces which have come from the depths. He occupies a very modest position. He is not himself the beauty of the crown; it has merely passed through him.

Klee goes on to discuss the dimensions

FIGTREE. 1929. *F. C. Schang Collection, New York.*

of a picture. In the world of art, nature is born again but is of necessity deformed, since it must submit to the specific dimensions of the plastic work of art. These dimensions are, in the first place, more or less limited formal factors such as the line, light and shade, and colour. The line is the most simple element of all; it relates only to measurement.... Tone value or, as it is also called, chiaroscuro, the numerous gradations between black and white— is somewhat different. In this case we are dealing with weight. A tone is charged with a greater or less amount of white or black energy. The third

131

element is the colours. Their nature cannot be understood either in terms of measurement or weight. If one compares two surfaces, the one pure yellow and the other pure red, of the same area and of equal luminosity, there is still a difference between them which we describe by the words 'yellow' and 'red'. Colours are 'qualities'. These formal elements—dimension, weight and quality—have certain interrelations. Colour is primarily quality, secondly, weight, because it has not only a chromatic value but also a degree of luminosity, and thirdly, dimension, because it has its limits, its extension. Tone value is, first and foremost, weight, but it is also dimensional in its extension and limitation. The line is purely dimensional.

This leads us to the first type of construction using the three categories of elements enumerated above. It is here that the centre of gravity of all our conscious work lies. If one is a master of the use of the medium one creates structures which have the power of attaining other and vaster dimensions. But if one's orientation in the field of form is inadequate, then the greatest and most important aspects of content cannot be attained, and the most exquisite qualities of soul cannot prevent a failure.

When the work in progress takes shape under our eyes we are tempted to give it, by association, a material interpretation. For any assemblage of forms in a complex structure may, with some imagination, be compared to things we know from nature. These associative qualities in the work are the origin of the heated misunderstandings between the artist and the public. Whereas the artist is entirely concerned to group the formal elements so precisely that each seems to fit inevitably into place, the uninstructed person looking over the painter's shoulder says the terrible words: 'But that isn't a bit like Uncle.' The artist, if his nerves are strong, says to

LATE. 1929. *F. C. Schang Collection, New York.*

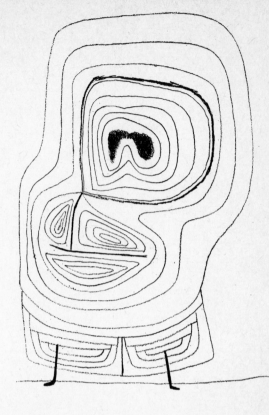

HEAVILY PREGNANT. 1934.

himself: "Uncle or no uncle, I must get on with my construction. . . . This new stone is perhaps a little too heavy—it puts too much weight on the left. I must put a counterweight on the right to redress the balance."

To the dimensions corresponding to the elementary plastic modes line, tonality, colour—there is added, through the constructive combination of these elements, the dimension of the organized form (*Gestalt*) or, if you like, the dimension of the object. To these dimensions yet another must be added; it is connected with 'content'.

"Certain relationships in the dimen-sions of lines", Klee goes on to explain, "the juxtaposition of certain tonalities, certain harmonies of colour, bring about certain well-defined and quite individual types of expression." For example, sharp zigzag movements set against a more horizontal line produce the effect of emotional contrast. "In the realm of tone value, contrasting expressions are obtained by the very extensive employment of all the tones from black to white (which ex-presses force, full inspiration and expiration) or by the employment of the bright upper register of the scale of tones or the employment of the

ILLUMINATED LEAF. 1929. *Klee-Stiftung, Berne.*

lower register, which is deep and sombre." As for the possible variations of content produced by colour combinations, they are innumerable. . . . Each organization of form, each combination has its own constructive expression, each organized form its own face, its own physiognomy. That

134

THE TWINS' PLACE. 1929. *Klee-Stiftung, Berne.*

is why pictures look at us, joyfully or severely, intense or relaxed, in comforting or forbidding mood, in sorrow or smiling.

But that is not all. These organized forms have their special 'attitude' or 'pose', which is the result of the way in which the various groups of elements have been set in motion. If a picture has a tranquil, stable pose and looks at its ease, that is because the aim has been to build not upwards but horizontally, or else, if we are dealing with a construction in height, to use the vertical element in a visible and systematic manner.

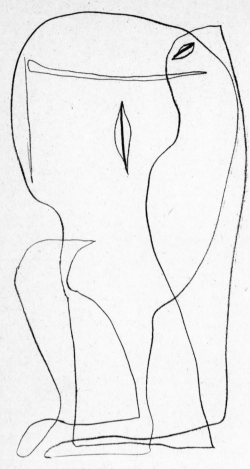

WARNING. 1935. *Klee-Stiftung, Berne.*

which is completely terrestrial. These animated, dynamic attitudes lead us on to the dimension of style. At this point Romanticism emerges in a peculiarly emotional form. This form of expression tries to soar higher and higher, to triumph more and more over the weight and bondage of terrestrial things. Thus one arrives at a form of Romanticism which merges with the universe. The static and dynamic parts of the mechanism of forms, therefore, coincide very accurately with the distinction between classical and romantic.

By this time the form arranged by the artist has gone through so many different and important dimensions that one can no longer call it a 'construction'. We can use a word rich in overtones: 'a composition'.

Klee then attempts to show how the artist comes to produce apparently arbitrary deformations of natural forms. His first reason is that he does not attribute to these forms the decisive importance which the 'realists' give them. He does not see in these finished, completed forms the essence of the creative process of nature. He is perhaps, without being clearly aware of it, a philosopher. The deeper his vision penetrates into things, the more inevitably he is faced not with the image of perfected nature but with creation's only essential image— 'genesis'. Looking forward into the future as he had looked back into the past and attributing duration to the process of genesis, he conceives the daring idea that the process of creation can today hardly be complete. He goes

This 'pose' is sometimes less rigid and is transported into an intermediary world—like water or the atmosphere—where (as in swimming or gliding) there are no longer any dominating verticals. It is a world unlike the world of the first attitude,

MONUMENT IN FERTILE COUNTRY. 1929.
Klee-Stiftung, Berne. →

further. He says to himself that, if we confine ourselves to the world below, then this world once looked quite different and will one day look different again. But then he looks beyond this world, and thinks there are perhaps other quite different forms on other stars. This ability to move about on the paths of creation is good training for the artist—it teaches him to be more mobile, more free to choose the paths traced by his creative activity.

A mere glance in the microscope suffices to show us what would seem fantastic images did we not know how they were revealed to us. Some people, coming across a reproduction like that in an *avant-garde* review, would exclaim in anger: "Are these natural forms? This is merely bad drawing." (This was a piece of malice on Klee's part, for some critics had employed exactly these terms when condemning his work.) To the question whether the artist must

ON AND IN THE LAKE. 1934. *Klee-Stiftung, Berne.*

138

DOUBLE FACE. 1933. *Felix Klee Collection, Berne.*

ACROBAT. 1930. *Felix Klee Collection, Berne.*

140

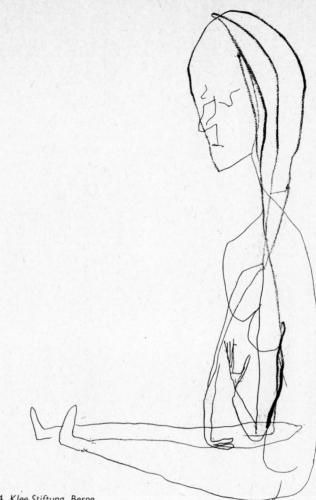

AND I SHALL SAY. 1934. *Klee Stiftung, Berne.*

therefore occupy himself with micro-
scopy and palaeontology, Klee replies:
"Only for the sake of making com-
parisons, only in the sense of mobility,
. . . only in the sense of liberty." One
must go from type to prototype. . . .
The true artists, those with a vocation,
are the ones who strive to approach

the secret depths where the prime
law fosters development and metamorphoses. What artist would not
wish to dwell where the central
factor of all temporal and spatial movement—what is known as the brain or
heart of creation—determines all
functions? in the very heart of nature,

GENTLE DRUMROLL. 1938. *Klee-Stiftung, Berne.*

at the source of all creation where the secret key to all is kept?

But there is no one rule—everyone must go where his heart leads him. Thus the Impressionists had the right to stick closely to the externals of nature, of daily life—to stay at ground level, so to speak. But as for us, our hearts force us into the depths.

But everything the artist brings back from his descents into these deep waters—whether they be called

142

WORLD HARBOUR. 1933. *Felix Klee Collection, Berne.*

143

dreams, ideas or fantasies, can only
be taken seriously if, in the course
of the organization of the work, they
are completely and adequately fused
in terms of plastic art. Then these
curiosities become realities, the realities of art, which add something to
life. Klee stresses the phrase about
'adequacy in terms of plastic art'. That
is what permits us to decide whether
we are dealing with works of art or
not and permits us to judge their
quality.

Ours is an agitated and confused age
but one can see in the artists of today
an effort to obtain purity in the modes
of expression in the plastic arts, and
rigour in their handling. Klee refers
to "the legend of the childishness of
my drawings", which is due to his
attempt to combine the representation
of an object or a man with the applica-
tion of the pure, linear element. An
attempt at realist representation would
have led to such a bewildering confusion of lines that it would have been
impossible to speak of purity of modes

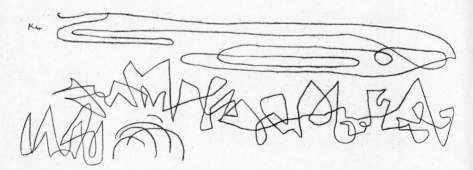

CLOUD ABOVE TREES. 1934. *Klee-Stiftung, Berne.*

HOVERING (ABOUT TO TAKE OFF). 1930. *Klee-Stiftung, Berne.*

of expression. Besides, Klee does not wish to show man as he is but as he might be. "Throughout the whole field of plastic techniques one must avoid contaminating the purity of technique—even when dealing with colours.

"Sometimes I dream of a work on a vast scale which would embrace the whole field of the elements of art, subject-matter, content and style", he adds. That will certainly remain a dream, but it is good to imagine the possibility. ·

Finally, he concludes, "we must not precipitate anything but let it ripen. We still lack supreme power; for the people are not yet on our side. But we are seeking a people and have made a beginning at the Bauhaus. We have begun with a community to which we give all we have. We can do no more."

The artist is isolated among men, the object sometimes of hostility—or worse—of indifference; in Klee's view he finds his true place only when face to face with nature, to which his work is tied by numerous bonds. The Jena lecture might be called a sort of Declaration of Rights of the Artist, not in relation to human society, but in relation to the society of natural objects, at the very heart of the Universe.

MORE WILL BE MARCHING SOON. 1934. *Klee-Stiftung, Berne.*

ROUGHHEWN HEAD. 1935. *F. C. Schang Collection, New York.*

EXPRESSIVE LYRE. 1935. *Klee-Stiftung, Berne.*

148

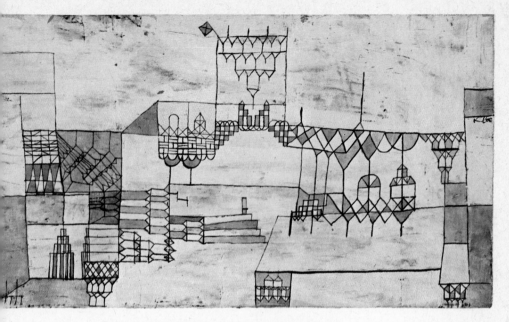

HALL OF SINGERS. 1930. *Private Collection, Berne.*

K. K. Gesellschaft

When, in November 1925, Otto Ralfs, who was an enthusiastic admirer of both Klee and Kandinsky, proposed the foundation of the K. K. Gesellschaft, which set itself the modest aim of obtaining for its members, for a small monthly payment, water-colours and paintings by the two artists, Klee was living in a villa in the upper part of Weimar while Kandinsky had a little furnished flat of two rooms and a kitchen in the old town. But their studios were next door to each other in the Bauhaus. As in Munich, where they had lived in the same street, they saw each other every day, and in the evening, together with their wives, met in Klee's house or at the theatre. Kandinsky frequently asked Klee to go to the cinema with him but only the name of Chaplin enticed Klee in. Apparently he was not greatly amused.

At Weimar, Klee to begin with still wore the slight fringe of beard which, according to Leopold Zahn, the author of the first small monograph on the painter, made him look like a figure from *The Burial of the Count d'Orgaz*.

Rolf Bürgi, who visited him along with his mother, tells us that the flat was pleasant and airy, with antique furniture. Water-colours hung on the

CONFUSED SIESTA. 1934. *Klee-Stiftung, Berne.*

walls. A black cat, which was the terror of Frau Kandinsky, sat enthroned on the sofa. After dinner, Klee took his violin and, accompanied by his wife, began to play Bach and Mozart. Next day they went to visit his studio. As they passed the theatre where Goethe had played the part of Orestes in *Iphigenia*, Klee amused them by mimicking some of Goethe's famous poses; this was one of his familiar jokes. The studio made a great impression on young Bürgi, who describes it as follows: "It was like an alchemist's laboratory. In the middle of it there were various easels and a chair. He was working simultaneously on several paintings. He spoke of his paintings with great simplicity: 'I had to do it like this so that the birds could sing.'" In fact in one of his water-colours dated 1922, now in the Museum of Modern Art, New York, he had invented a 'twittering machine', *Die Zwitschermaschine* (Cat. 40). Although she was not able to acquire the *Zwitschermaschine*, Frau Bürgi insisted on acquiring *The Bird Caller* (page 69),

150

TOWARDS THE MOUNTAINS. 1934. *Klee-Stiftung, Berne.*

151

a delicious work, all in transparent
tones. In the bird with its long pointed
beak it was not difficult to recognize
the art dealer, Flechtheim, who owned
a well-known Berlin gallery.

In Dessau, where the Bauhaus
moved in 1926, the two artists lived
in the two wings of a small house built
by Gropius. Klee had seven rooms;
Kandinsky had only four, since he had
no children. His part of the house was
finished first so that he was able to
offer Klee hospitality for some time.
Dessau was certainly not a gracious
residential city. When Gropius called
a meeting of the professors of the
Weimar Bauhaus to discuss with the
Bürgermeister of Dessau the conditions
on which the new school would be
built, their wives discovered a stretch
of forest on the outskirts of the city
and suggested to their husbands that
they should advise the municipality,
which did not know where to house
the professors, to appropriate a piece
of virgin land.

Kandinsky and Klee took a certain
amount for their own small gardens,
which were not separated in any way.
But although the artists and their
families were so closely united, the
gardens seemed to be divided by an
invisible fence. Klee never set foot in
Kandinsky's garden without being
invited; Kandinsky never set foot in
Klee's. When they were busy in the
garden they behaved as if they were
concealed from each other by the
invisible fence—a mode of behaviour
which greatly surprised Nina Kandinsky
who watched the scene from her
balcony. Nina Kandinsky was a Russian

FRUIT. 1930. *Private Collection, Berne.*

153

EMIGRATING. 1933. *Klee-Stiftung, Berne.*

of these years, which for Kandinsky were the most exciting of his life and for Klee the most fertile. She remembered the parties in Klee's house and the lively evenings in her own when Klee was there with his wife and the other professors. One evening, when there was dancing, Klee turned up with a turban which brought out his Oriental looks. It seemed as if all his life he had worn a turban—the head-dress most suited to wizards and maharajas.

The more intimate musical evenings were all held at the Klees' and were very simple in the old German style. On these occasions Klee was purely a musician, intent on Bach, Beethoven, Handel, Haydn and Mozart. He played almost every evening after supper with his wife. Then in bed he read his French and Greek authors. But when he was possessed by music · it was impossible to talk to him about poetry or painting. His son, Felix, took advantage of this fact.

The two families often spent the evening together. In good weather they saw each other rather less because the Kandinskys liked to go cycling in the shade of the trees. Klee himself preferred to walk; he said that on foot one could observe things better.

In summer the two families separated for the holidays. In 1924 Klee was in Sicily; in 1926 in Italy again, visiting Elba, Florence, Pisa and Ravenna. In 1927 and 1928 he was in France, Brittany and Corsica. In December 1928 the K. K. Gesellschaft provided the money to pay for a trip to Egypt where he stayed for a month.

from Moscow. She had lived through the Revolution and this extraordinarily scrupulous sense of individual property disturbed her deeply. But in fact the two painters were behaving as if they were painting side by side, each intent on his own work.

Nina Kandinsky has often spoken

BARK CULTURE. 1935. *Felix Klee Collection, Berne.*

Picturesque Egypt—the Egypt of mosques and suks—he did not like. It did not correspond to what he had imagined. Egypt he found only in the pure geometric tracery of its monuments, in the flow of its sand and water, in the pale light of its sky saturated with colour. It was to remain one of the deep underlying themes of Klee's sensibility—one of which he had had a presentiment (*Blue Mountain*, 1919). Later he was to write to Lily: "I am painting a landscape [*Monument in a Fertile Land*, 1929] rather like the view from the top of the cliffs in the Valley of the Kings looking towards the orchard lands." But he did not only skim over these flat fields with their network of vertical and horizontal parallels (*Highway and Byways*, 1929); through the mouths of the tombs, he slipped into a subterranean world peopled by spirits, by which he would be haunted to the end of his life.

But the Spring the two painters celebrated together. They would go in an open carriage to Wörlitzpark. It was a long road lined with lilacs; the horses' pace was slow and the air mild and scented. For Nina Kandinsky the whole poetry of life was in that drive, which perhaps reminded her of Chekhov's Russia. The two ladies sat together with the men opposite them. Klee kept thinking of Goethe, who had so often driven this way.

One of the great events of these years was in 1928, when Kandinsky, assisted by Felix Klee, made his first experiment in staging opera with Mussorgsky's *Pictures in an Exhibition*, which Mussorgsky had composed in 1874, drawing his inspiration from the pictures of his friend Hartmann. Kandinsky had designed the scenes, which were all abstract and geometric and thus went clean against the character of the music which was undeniably Impressionistic. But although

HARBOUR AT K. 1939. *Klee-Stiftung, Berne.*

156

EMACHT. 1932. *Felix Klee Collection, Berne.*

he did violence to the music in one sense, in another he thereby liberated it, since to have stuck to Impressionist scenography would inevitably have spoiled the effect of the music. But this was clearly not the only reason for Klee's enthusiasm. Kandinsky had made it possible for him, as it were, to see *music*. But had not Klee himself already attempted to transcribe it, to translate it into line, in his drawings in the year 1927? In the *Hall of Singers*

from the Bürgi collection, his memories of his journeys to Sicily and Egypt enabled him to produce work as light and airy as a Mozart aria.

In December 1932, Kandinsky, who was worried by the political events in Germany, decided to leave Dessau for good although he had applied for and obtained German nationality. Klee had left a year before, preferring—as he said in a moment of temper—the more modest professors of the

157

DRAWING FOR "PIERETTE". 1937. *Klee-Stiftung, Berne.*

DRAWING FOR ITINERANT CIRCUS. 1937. *Private Collection, U.S.A.*

Academy at Düsseldorf, to which he had been appointed, to the geniuses of the Bauhaus. Since he was unable to find a flat in Düsseldorf, his life was divided between the two towns.

"We dined in silence at Paul Klee's", Nina Kandinsky relates. "His wife had fallen ill and had been taken to hospital a few days previously. Felix, who was beginning to have considerable success as a producer—he had studied production at the Bauhaus—was away for professional reasons. We sat there, the three of us alone, round the table. The pain of separation after so many years of life together caught at our throats. I was less upset when I left Russia with Kandinsky. The two artists had been brought together by life and by their careers. Daily contact

THE LITTLE PRUSSIAN. 1938. *Klee-Stiftung, Berne.*

and a carefully regulated intimacy on either side had united them. But. can one go on to say that this exemplary friendship corresponded to an affinity of mind and that the bonds between them are to be found in their work? Pierre Volboudt has the following comment to make:

"They were separated by a fundamental antinomy which—their art apart—pointed to a fundamentally different concept of the world. In the one it was analytic and lost itself in a confusion of meanings, allusions and symbols. In the other it was synthetic, expansive and source of radiation.

160

GARDEN GATE M. 1932. *R. Doetsch-Benziger Collection, Basle.*

"For Klee art was always cast 'in the image of creation'; but this image is a parody of reality—a poetic travesty. It is perpetually being reduced to absurdity and deformed in order to make of it something else. Everything is ambiguous, masked behind the outward appearance of animal or plant, of faceless powers, which are fluid, mobile and unresolved. In order that it may stalk and surprise nature in its various metamorphoses the human disguises itself in nature. The artist rummages in Creation's property box. There is nothing which does not serve him, nothing which does not come into his

161

CHILDREN'S PLAYGROUND. 1937.

game—art and its oldest remnants such as inscriptions, mosaics, Assyrian tablets, cracked pottery, imaginary ideograms, graffiti; nature with its various processes and chance effects—its striations, strata and maculations, the slow wear of time which in the thinnest fragment of rock imitates the work of the human hand. The hand, in its turn, Klee said, must be 'the instrument of a distant past'.

"Kandinsky's work, on the other hand, is outside of time, for it dispenses with Creation and its works. Man is absent from it. One might even wonder whether it was made for him. If it is destined for him, in accordance with the painter's wish, it is in order to educate him by means of an *askesis*, which is perhaps derived from ancient rites—the only trace of the past in the master of absolute art—and which is intended to teach him to dispense with appearances.

"Kandinsky's work does not relate anything, nor does it evoke anything.

OH! BUT OH! 1937. *Private Collection, Berne.*

Klee's *Märchen*, on the contrary, are merely the setting for an event and often that event itself. Plants and geometry, even, appear on the stage and have their part to play. Space progresses in planes, unrolls in vague parallels, undulates and climbs. A quivering sensibility seems to run through his line and animate even abstraction.

"In Kandinsky's strict *formations* one finds only a formal sensibility. To the end he retained a power which was always to hand. His final productions were to be festivals of the imagination, caprices of invention which were at once extremely free and extremely controlled.

"His work arose outside anything that exists. Because of this haughty rejection of all that is, it does not belong to any world. It is a world of its own, which has nothing to do with the one in which we live.

"Klee was suspicious of the effects of too prolonged a state of consciousness. He had to keep to that intermediary realm where everything changes and changes itself, ramifies infinitely into equivocation and bifurcates into inextricability. He was careful not to lose anything his eyes spelt out—no detail, no unevenness, no sign. In his last works everything comes back to the sign. He draws only his great hasty, summary marks, his allegorical skeletons, which are the vocabulary of those obscure regions where the occult veils the visible and reveals only the ghost of things; it is the enigma which baffles all combinations for the painter has, perhaps designedly, scrambled the secret cipher."

DARING. 1932. *Klee-Stiftung, Berne.*

GARDEN RHYTHM. 1932. *Felix Klee Collection, Berne.*

Crystalline Painting

We have already said that, in spite of the great revelation of Kairouan, Klee preferred water-colour and certain alchemies of his own to oils. Even during the Bauhaus period, which is considered the happiest of his life and career, his works are small in dimension. The *Botanical Theatre* begun in 1924 and finished only ten years later, which was considered a large-scale work measures only $19\frac{5}{8}'' \times 26''$. It was only after his return to Berne, when he had a presentiment of death, that Klee dared to face the challenge of large surfaces—large for him, that is to say, but relatively modest compared with those of Picasso or Matisse. His last work, which was found after his death, was barely sketched on a large sheet of paper and was not more than five feet by just over three feet. In spite of the vast studios put at his disposal in Weimar, Dessau and Düsseldorf, he was still a cabinet painter.

In almost all the works he painted between 1920 and 1923 the graphic element predominates.

Klee, who drew equally well with either hand, had trained his hands to an

MONOLOGUE OF A KITTEN. 1938. *Felix Klee Collection, Berne.*

166

SCENE WITH BIRDS. 1937. *Klee-Stiftung, Berne.*

extraordinary degree—indeed he believed that one of the principal aims of artistic education was to develop great manual skill. As an inevitable result, his hands drew automatically, independently of his will, and would have become the blind instrument of his feelings had his reason not intervened at a certain point and given meaning to the creative act.

Klee's researches in the field of form are always accurate and careful. He could explain his pictures to his pupils as if (their content and poetic feeling apart) they were equations. Yet Klee does not fall into formalism. On the contrary, he was so closely bound up with reality that one of his most penetrating interpreters, Georg Schmidt, has described him as "the most realistic painter of the twentieth century".

Will Grohmann has classified the works of the period under discussion as follows: "There are those which have their place at the centre of

167

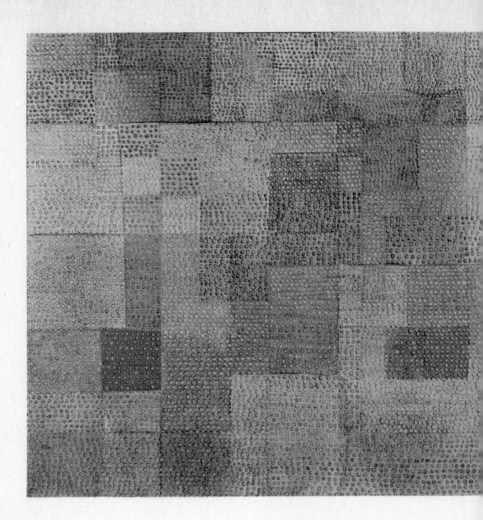

POLYPHONY. 1932. *Emanuel Hoffman-Stiftung, Kunstmuseum, Basle.*

his activity and those which lie on the periphery. In the former, Klee's attitude to the universe finds symbolical expression. The pictorial phenomenon resists analysis. One can only give a partial explanation of it by comparing the pictures with other works or by tracing the course of the artist's development. One cannot separate subject or theme from the act of genesis or from its formal development. Taken as a whole, these works are remote from nature, if that term is at all applicable. One can hardly talk of abstraction. For Klee it is less a question of the subject's *existence* than of its *nature*. We might call them—as he himself does—crystalline.

"In an intermediary group, form and sense emerge from interwoven elements and formal signs, which have a certain depth of meaning but do not attain to the rank of symbols. In the peripheral category we must place those pictures which deal with a fleeting study of phenomena from Nature or from life and which have, as a starting-point, a given situation, not an internal image. Klee always sees things in the perspective of the totality, the entire range of formal and creative possibilities. Thus the concept of totality applies to all his work.

"This classification holds good for a period of ten years; but in Dessau the paintings in the third group are already beginning to be superseded. They might be said to fall into the second category. The personal element, which had never had more than a relative importance, disappears and is replaced

169

by a kind of detachment which projects on a background of general truth the interest Klee felt in all existence. The dividing lines between the categories become more and more indistinct. They now refer to a variation in method or execution and not to a scale of values. In the peripheral category we also find masterpieces. They are not less great—merely different, just as the autobiographical works of the great poets are different from the rest but are still spirit of their spirit. Where the artist ceases to explore the depths we find compensations in different powers, which give the picture its true value."

But to whichever group the work belongs, the artist always proceeds like a musician "who writes note after note and passing from motive to theme, from one theme to another, develops both".

The values of the artist's sensibility are translated into tonal values; they group themselves into harmonies, grow into themes, develop as variations, swell into crescendos, branch out into parallel, rising rhythms, vibrate in high notes.

When he was complimented on one of his works, Klee parried by saying: "The miracle of this little painting is entirely due to the fact that the brush with which I painted it had *three* hairs—not one more nor less than I needed." Certainly at this period Klee worked as much with the pen as

POND WITH SWANS. 1937. *Mrs. John Rockefeller, New York.*

ANIMALS IN THE PADDOCK. 1938. *F. C. Schang Collection, New York.*

with the brush. His pictures are often simple coloured designs, either figurative or abstract. The Chinese were his models whether he was using horizontal strokes as in *A Leaf from the Town Records* (page 106), or an undulating line, as in *Untamed Waters* (page 198), or a hooked line as in *Little Picture of Cubes*, 1925 (page 81). At other times there is the incisive line of the etchings *Seven Blossoms*, 1926. French Divisionism is reduced to a game of draughtsmanship—severely linear in *Ad Parnassum* (Cat. 97) and fantastically geometrical in *Barbarian Captain* (page 181). In *Picture of a Park* (page 203), the colour seems to leap out from the gay whirl of the paint. Finally the famous 'embroideries', inspired by Oriental carpets, are graphic compositions, as are obviously the ideograms and the 'signs' which mark the artist's last period.

It was only at the end of his long stay in Germany that, having mastered the problem of colour, he returned to the problem of materials, which he had faced and successfully solved in the 'magic squares' of the Weimar days. The supreme beauty of the 'squares' is due, in fact, to the austere density of the pigments and the wonderful resonance of the harmonies, which contrast with the mathematical clarity of the design. The latter may be immobile, as in *Table of Colour in Grey Major* (page 130) in the Klee Foundation or shot with light, the source of all

171

FREE BUT SECURELY HELD. 1930. *F. C. Schang Collection, New York.*

movement, as in *Blossoming* (Cat. 109).

Klee's colour, which in many of his works is merely an opaque background on which his subject is graphically rendered, and in others has the limpid transparency of glass or a brilliant gleaming quality, in the 'magic squares' is a noble medium. So too it was in the 1938 pastels. Klee's mysticism and sensuality fuse perfectly in these sub-lime abstract harmonies, which have had such a great influence on modern painting. It is in the 'magic squares' that Klee reveals himself as one of the greatest painters of his time, thus justifying eight years after Kairouan (the first example is dated 1922) the proud statement he made there: "I and colour are one." That is to say he rediscovered that poetry in the

172

LAGOON CITY. 1932. *Private Collection, Berne.* →

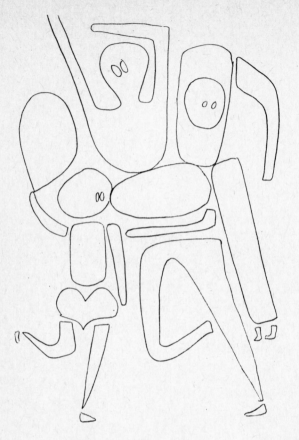

ACROBATS EXERCISING.
1938. *Felix Klee Collection, Berne.*

artist's materials which had so moved
him at Pompeii during his first stay in
Italy. "They seem to have been painted
and discovered specially for me",
he had said of the Pompeian frescoes.
In those cases where the 'magic
squares' do not give the physical
sensation of fresco work, they have
the intensity of coloured glass, the
gaiety of enamels, the jewelled luminosity of a mosaic.

The works of the period 1930 to 1933,
on the other hand, recall—as far as the
media employed are concerned—the
effects he obtained at the beginning of
his career with the famous 'sous-
verres'. Examples are *Nekropolis* (Cat.
92) and *The Man of the Future* (Cat. 104),
in which some people claimed to see
the man with the swastika. In spite of
the power of their drawing, these
works make their impression through
the way in which the pigment is applied
by nervous strokes of the palette knife.

SHIPWRECKED.
1938. *Klee-Stiftung, Berne.*

In *Young Tree* (1932), the buds are painted in relief; the contrast with the light arabesque of the tree gives a feeling of imminent, magic vitality. In a landscape from nature, the pink and violet *Trees in October* (Cat. 94), the tufts of the trees are obtained by thick brushwork; the results remind one of the technique so much discussed today in 'tachiste' and 'fluid' painting.

Klee looks upon his sheet of paper as a stage—a setting for a spectacle inspired by nature or a purely imaginary entertainment. But there can be no play without characters, and in Klee the characters are varied and numerous. In this essentially magic production the characters may also be objects which the artist distributes in space and humanizes, as he did with the fish when he was a child. His characters take him back to the theatre —and he did indeed paint many scenes

175

MODEL OF A FLOWER VASE. 1930. *Herman Rupf Collection, Berne.*

176

OPEN. 1933. *Felix Klee Collection, Berne.*

and characters either tragic or grotesque from theatre and circus in Weimar. Sometimes the light comes from within; sometimes it comes from without like lamplight. Oftener it comes from both directions at once as in *Ventriloquist—Man shouting in a Bog* (Cat. 46).

In the thirteen years which concern us here, nature plays a great part in Klee's work. He stages enchanted impromptus or humoresques—often both together. As we have seen he may choose the disguise of a Chinese décor as in *View of a Mountain Sanctuary*. From this time on however the artist is more and more interested in the problems of space and form which took him further and further away from the images of the external world. Yet both form and space are conceived poetically and sometimes symbolically as well.

177

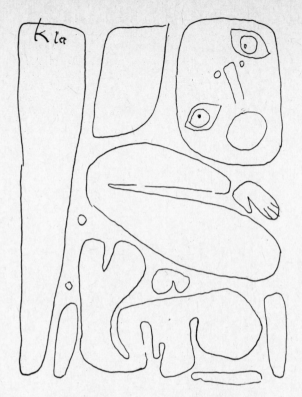

OUTBURST OF FEAR. 1939. *Klee-Stiftung, Berne.*

Reduplication of form gives us *Hanging Fruits* (Cat. 34), *Dying Plants* (Cat. 41), *Dream City*, 1921, and so on. Other forms seemed to be directly generated by space—flying forms like *Extended Surfaces*, flying and symbolical forms like *Twins* (Cat. 83) and *Diane*, 1931. Space also gives rise to a play with constructions—sometimes purely in terms of perspective as in *Perspective of a Room with Inmates* (Cat. 33), sometimes with a metaphysical flavour as in *Uncomposed Object in Space* (Cat. 75).

Space generates abstract rhythms as in the 'magic squares' and in the pictures painted after his trip to Egypt such as *Individualistic Measurement of the Beds* (Cat. 93), *The Sun sweeps the Plain* (Cat. 74), or in the masterpiece of the series *Highway and Byways* which beautifully sums up the artist's researches into line and colour.

Lastly, we must consider the graphic and ideographic forms, the forms and characters which give a foretaste of the artist's last period, when he was

SUCCESSFUL INCANTATION. 1937. *Rosengart Collection, Lucerne.*

once again strongly attracted by
Islam—partly owing to his heredity,
partly because of a peculiar piritual
inclination towards it.

Klee's work astonishes by the
variety of its themes and techniques,
by its revelation of a universe which
otherwise only poetry and music have
touched, by its sensibility and fantasy.
Klee's fantasy is beyond all doubt
musical. But it is the purely plastic
qualities of Klee's work which force
themselves upon the attention of
modern artists, a large number of
whom have drawn upon its rich
resources. One need mention only
two of the most genuine and original
among them: Wolds and de Stael, both
of them dead before their time. The
roots of their work lie in Klee's
achievement.

BARBARIAN CAPTAIN. 1932 →
Felix Klee Collection, Berne.

ORGELBERG. 1934. *Private Collection, Berne.*

ARCHITECTURE IN RUINS. 1938. *Klee-Stiftung, Berne.*

182

FALL. 1938. *Klee-Stiftung, Berne.*

Return to Berne

One could write ten books on Klee
with entirely different texts and
publish ten entirely different volumes
of reproductions. The phenomenon
'Klee' is as vast as it is complex and
its ramifications are almost inextric-
able. "We can never claim", said his
friend and biographer, Will Grohmann,
"to embrace it in its totality and
multiplicity."

Grohmann got to know Klee in
Weimar at a point when, having left
his circle of friends in Munich, he was
disposed to welcome new acquaint-

ances who were interested in his
painting. "I came just at the right
time," Grohmann continues, "for I
wanted to see his drawings, a lot of his
drawings—which was a thing no one
ever asked for. No one wanted to
exhibit them and he did not want to
sell them, because—as he said—they
formed part of his equipment. To him
they were, so to speak, archives of
his plastic invention.

"First of all I wrote an essay on these
drawings, followed by several articles
and in 1929 by a book published in
Paris by the 'Cahiers d'Art'. In 1933 I
published a volume on the drawings and

DOCUMENT. 1933. *Angela Rosengart Collection, Lucerne.*

later the biography, which appeared in 1954. But I always feel that I did not sufficiently stress the inexhaustible richness of his work and personality— that I merely hinted at.

"When I think of Klee and of our work 'in common' as he wrote one day with his habitual modesty, the memory of hours passed together rises up in my memory—hours like his paintings, full of sweetness, tranquil gaiety and spiritual intensity. One could speak to him about anything—even personal matters. But when the subject did not affect him, he listened with a kind of indifferent attention.

"He spoke little and liked to be silent. When he did speak a few words he selected them and used them, like the lines in his pictures, only after due reflection. In his talk, as in his letters, he had certain key words which were pointers to the trend of his thought. When he was thinking of having his drawings published he wrote an oblique letter with a pun on the word 'publisher', which was a hint that I had to find him one. A publisher was at last discovered but only one out of three volumes was brought out because in the meantime barbarism had broken out in Germany. It was these drawings which brought us together. I was fascinated by their construction. They were exactly like his handwriting; later I saw that in his manner, his gestures, his expressions and his language the man was in perfect harmony with his work.

"A slight veil floated over both Klee and his work. He had become unused to the 'direct approach' although he had employed it in his youth. But this veil was not used to hide things—it was there to make people look more closely. For what else is the meaning of the word 'schema', which I have applied to the successive forms he invented? It means precisely that shrouding of the spiritual perspective which Klee renders directly visible.

"When we looked at his work together, he would never attempt to lead me astray but helped me with a suggestive phrase and then waited for approval or criticism.

"'What a nightmare' he said when we were faced by a confused scene, or 'How it soars' when the picture dealt with flying forms. In the case of the *Ageing Venus*, he merely gave a sidelong smile and said that it was his contribution to the *chronique scandaleuse* and only for initiates.

"It is easier to understand the Klee of the hermetic works today than it was in 1920. New aspects of his work were always emerging, full of enigmas, and a great deal of time had to pass before it became clear that Klee started from plastic formulae in order to arrive at the object and not vice versa. These formulae he found in play and in reality, in his relations with the universe. which for him, as for musicians, was to be found in relations and functions.

"We understood each other from the first moment we met. It seemed to both of us that we had known each other for a long time. We had the same preferences in art—El Greco, for example, whom he would have collected, he said, had he been a millionaire; Rembrandt's drawings and Islamic ornament. But here too Klee limited himself to one or two hints. One never got further than 'allusions'.

"When, in 1940, the year of his death, he felt the illness which was to carry him off some months later, progressing, he wrote to me after reading the *Oresteia*: 'I have just made the acquaintance of Tragedy; it is not by chance that I have set out along the Tragic Way.'

SCHOŁAR. 1933. *Private Collection, Berne.*

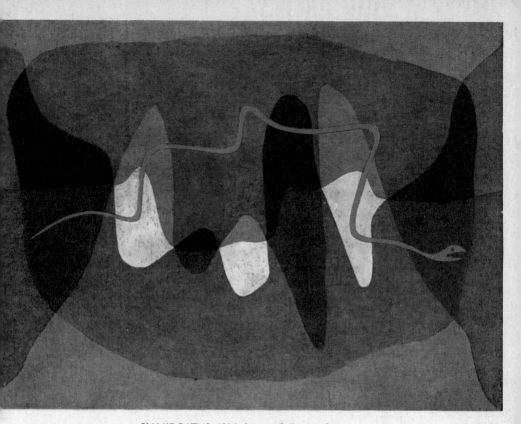

SNAKE PATHS. 1924. *Private Collection, Berne.*

"Only work made him perfectly happy. 'What happiness there could be in a couple of lines!' he wrote to me shortly before the publication of his drawings. He liked best to be in his studio.

"Once he wrote to me that he did not wish to be too easily understood. 'I shall shortly let you have some nuts worth cracking', he added. When something I had written pleased him he would thank me by giving me one of his works. Thus one day he sent me a drawing with a note which ran: 'An example of the kind of little animal I breed.' Thus he belittled the importance of his present.

"He was always concentrated in himself. Hence his measured movements, his slow pace and his considered speech. He seemed so indolent that it was a surprise, on revisiting him after three or four weeks, to see the number of paintings, drawings and sketches he had finished. This was possible, because, if he was not disturbed, he could work very hard. The only interruption allowed was for

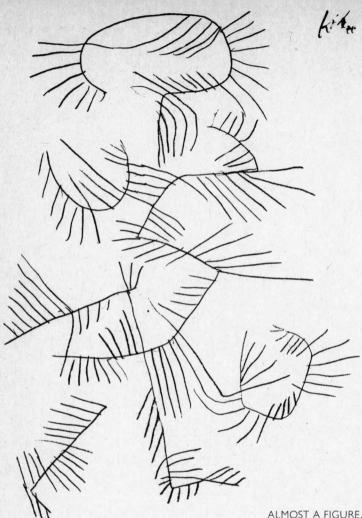

ALMOST A FIGURE. 1938. *Klee-Stiftung, Berne.*

music, which he looked on as part of his work, or at least as a preparation for his work. He enjoyed music greatly but he also needed it as a stimulant. It went deeper than painting, he felt, had a more profound tradition and was an unending source of instruction. He saw in Bach and Mozart his true masters, saying that they had taught him more than any great master of painting. And the sequence of his 'schemas' which emerge from each other or are contrasted with each other, derive from his wide knowledge of the rules

PATHOS. 1938. *Felix Klee Collection, Berne.*

YOUNG TREE (CHLORANTHEMUM). 1932. *Private Collection, Berne.*

of music. In his work we find the technique of the exposition of themes, of their succession, fusion and development. Thus Klee realized his youthful dream of being a musician in a strange way. In painting he was the musician he had dreamt of being."

When Klee appeared in Berne and said to Rolf Bürgi, son of the first collector of his works: "Here I am, there's no place for me in Germany any more", there were few people in his native town who had heard of him, although he had exhibited in New York and Paris and his name was already famous. Frau Bürgi set about making him better known and appreci-

ated. Will Grohmann was invited to give the inhabitants of Berne an idea of Klee's work; but the great retrospective exhibition was not held until 1935.

Klee had arrived in Berne unexpectedly. After his dismissal from the academy at Düsseldorf he had left everything behind him in fear of his life. Yet up to the last he had resisted Lily's insistence that he must not have any illusions about the Nazis. But he had, after all, once written in his Diary: "What would I be without Germany?"

Rolf Bürgi went north to remove the works which had been left in the

AMATEUR DRUMMER. 1940. *Private Collection.*

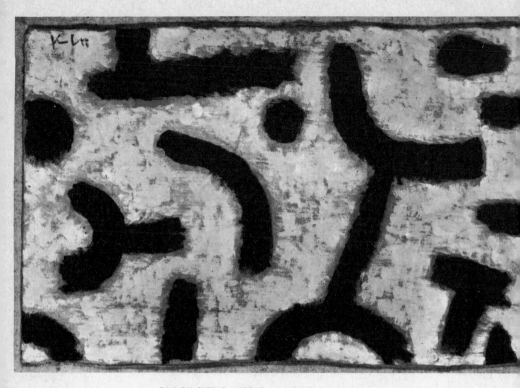

BLACK SIGNS. 1938. *Felix Klee Collection, Berne.*

studio in Düsseldorf and returned to Berne with Frau Klee, who was no longer the authoritarian Lily of old days. She was a firm believer in her husband's genius and was full of admiration and attention; now she lived only for him.

All the money the artist had earned and banked in Germany was lost. Klee was back once more in the state he had been in when he left Berne thirty years before. Then he had been poor but rich in illusions; now he was poor but rich in experience as an artist and in his world-wide fame. The generosity of Frau Bürgi succeeded in interesting some people in Klee. She had been the first person in Switzerland to believe in his genius at a time when his own father had doubts. "I am not saying that he has no talent," the old man had muttered in his beard, "but he doesn't take enough care over what he does." The municipal authorities however remained indifferent to the eloquence of Will Grohmann.

Convinced that he would never be

POISON. 1932 *Klee-Stiftung, Berne.*

BROKEN MASK. 1934. *Felix Klee Collection, Berne.*

able to return to Germany, Klee decided to ask for Swiss citizenship. His request was received with suspicion. One councillor opposed it energetically because, so he maintained, he had seen a picture by Klee which was particularly damaging to Switzerland. It was a painting of a little field with too many cows in it. "Art of this kind does us harm. People abroad will say that we have not sufficient pasture for our cattle."

Perhaps this is a case of *ben trovato*. Many years before when Arp had asked for Swiss citizenship he had been told: "Your art will lead you to the lunatic asylum and we will have to pay for your keep and the treatment which will be lavished upon you." Arp gave up the attempt. But Klee insisted. Finally, however, Swiss citizenship was granted to him. Too late—he had died the day before as a German in a nursing home near Locarno.

← DIANA IN THE AUTUMN WIND. 1934. *Klee-Stiftung, Berne.*

195

NOT PLEASED. 1939. *Klee-Stiftung, Berne.*

196

LITTLE BAROQUE BASKET. 1939. *Klee-Stiftung, Berne.*

Angels, Saints and Demons

When he came back to Berne Klee had still seven years to live. It was not until three years later—in 1936—that he began to doubt his ability to stand up to the disease which had begun to make itself felt. But in 1933 he was barely fifty-four and full of life. Admittedly the flight from Germany as a result of the Nazis' threats had shaken him severely. Germany was the country which had once understood him, which had given him a wife, a home, a professorship and a model—Goethe. But the new Germany did not know what to do with Goethes. It wanted peoples to subject and living space to rule. Any art which did not exalt these aims was considered degenerate. One hundred of Klee's works were confiscated by the Nazis.

As he had done in Weimar, Klee examined his conscience carefully and asked himself whether he had really achieved what he had set out to do. Up to 1936 he contented himself with finishing some works already begun—at least in his mind—and with bringing quietly to a close a great epoch in his life.

197

UNTAMED WATERS. 1934. *Private Collection, Berne.*

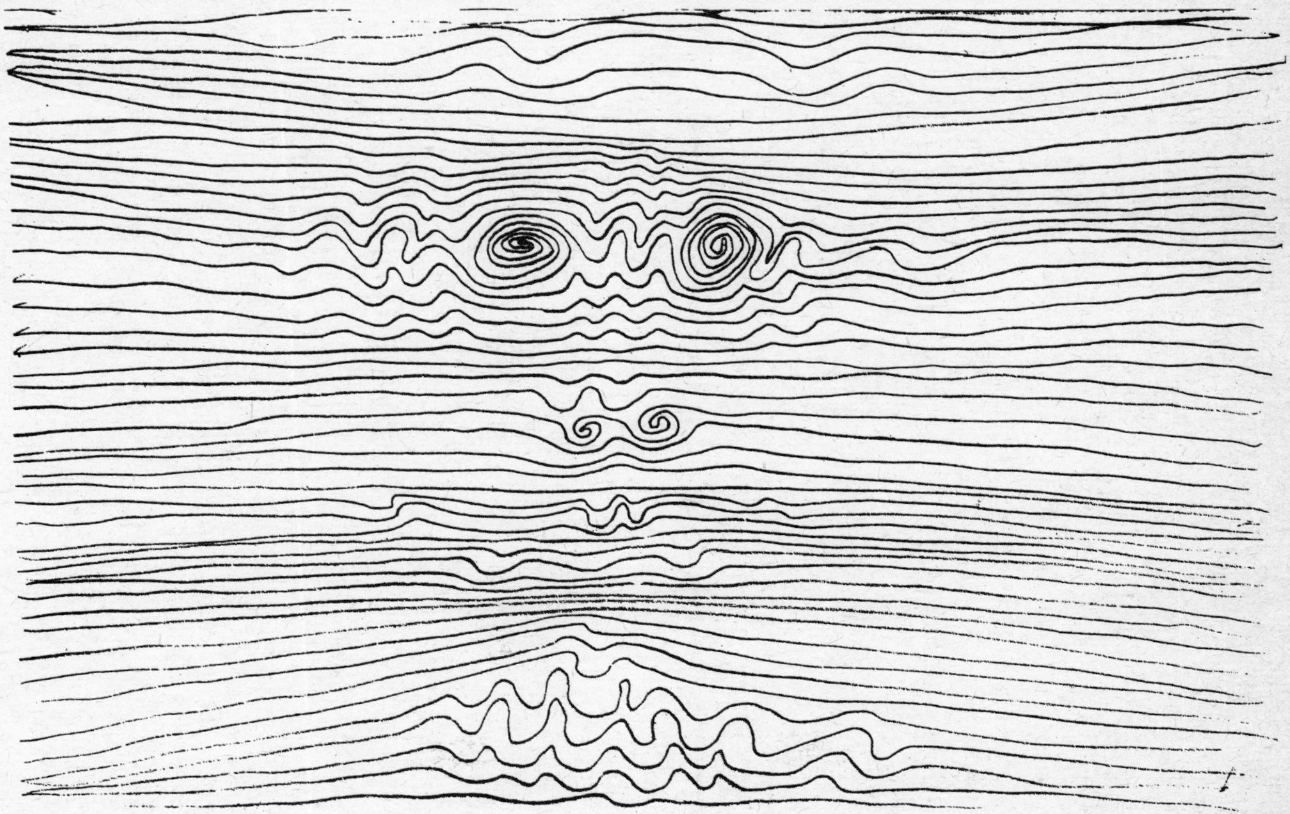

199

GAME ON THE WATER. 1935. *Klee-Stiftung, Berne.*

HOW LIKE AN ANGEL. 1939. *Klee-Stiftung, Berne.*

He ought to have been satisfied; but he was not. *Broken Mask* (page 195) already expresses his suffering of spirit. It is a water-colour with nothing in common with his previous work—a cry of pain and fear in the night.

Many other works are successful restatements of his favourite themes: *Diana in the Autumn Wind* (page 194) and *Dame Demon* (Cat. 112) are figures he already knew, symbols which were already familiar. *Gate of the Deserted Garden* (page 206) and *The Way Out Discovered* (page 202) rounded off previous experiences without adding anything to them.

But in that same year, 1935, the first signs of the conflict which was to torment him appeared in two completely different pictures: *Rough-hewn Head* (page 147) and *Two Fruit Landscape* (page 209). The former is a sculptural

FORGETFUL ANGEL. 1939. *Klee-Stiftung, Berne.*

form, firm and geometrical in its classicism; the latter a decidedly Expressionist work. The artist seems to be hesitating; but Expressionism would win the day.

So in Berne Klee came back to the Expressionist tendencies which had marked the beginning of his career. But it was no longer the academic expression of the early etchings. The Expressionism of his last period is both formal and symbolical and points the way to universal and religious concepts.

It is difficult to say how much his illness influenced this new orientation. Certainly it becomes increasingly difficult to find echoes of Mozart or Bach in his work. Now it is the turn of modern music with the tortured beat of the drums and sometimes—as in the disenchanted *Insula dulcamara* (Cat. 140)—the humour of the saxophone.

THE WAY OUT AT LAST. 1935. *Felix Klee Collection, Berne.*

Klee was ill now. Following an attack of measles, he developed sclerodermia which slowly dried up his mucous membranes. It is noticeable that in his drawings the line loses its boldness and brio; it no longer accords with Henri Michaux's definition of it as "une ligne pour le plaisir d'etre ligne, d'aller, ligne". No doubt it obeys the artist's will but has no longer its old Mozartean lightness. The artist's imagination turned more and more to 'signs' which have 'a sematic value, like the Chinese characters in the *Book of Metamorphoses*'. His favourite colours are yellows, greens, blues and reds, which are at first luminous but later become increasingly sombre and thick.

In 1937 and 1938 the artist at last faced the challenge of large canvasses without, however, giving up his own brand of alchemy. He mixed gum and chalk as he prepared the canvas, alternating smooth and rough surfaces by sticking on pieces of packing paper, gauze or newspaper; when he painted he mixed all techniques—oil, tempera

202

PICTURE OF A PARK. 1933 *Felix Klee Collection, Berne.*

DOUBLE ISLAND. 1939. *Klee-Stiftung, Berne.*

204

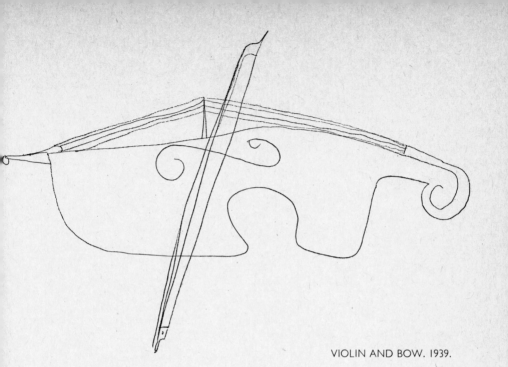

VIOLIN AND BOW. 1939.

and water-colour. He also used pastels a great deal because of their soft sensual quality.

After his return to Berne, then, we have chiefly works which are complementary to what went before. Towards 1937 the first great pastels appear with their luminous, tender backgrounds, which are sometimes plain, sometimes constructed like tiled work on which are traced certain signs; these are at first light, but later they become increasingly powerful and weighty. It is almost as if the artist himself were beating a drum like his *Drummer*. These 'signs' imitate Islamic script or notes of music or else allude to architectural forms, both round and angular. Sometimes they hint at the outline of a human figure as in *Pomona* (page 247).

The graphic Expressionism of 1937 and 1938 is succeeded by the figurative Expressionism of the years 1939 to 1940. Figures of angels and devils betray the artist's fear of death. Of these pictures some are barbarous, some refined; but they do not express the extreme agony which we find in the last works of all.

In 1939, feeling that the end was near, he gave up even the short drives in an open carriage which Rolf Bürgi had persuaded him to take. That year he painted two thousand works. He was living on the second floor of a small house in the Kistlerweg in Berne. In front of the house there

GATE OF THE DESERTED GARDEN. 1935. *Private Collection, Berne.*

was a little garden with a pine tree—the faithful pine which had accompanied him from childhood and which was one of his most trusty symbols.

In the summer, he received a visit from Kandinsky. Two years previously Braque and Picasso had come to see him. Kandinsky found him in bed; to cheer him up he invited him to Paris. The sick man raised his hand a little and made a slight negative gesture; but his head lay sunk in the pillows. His eyes said that they would not see each other again.

The pictures painted in 1940 occupy an extremely important place in the corpus of his work.

In *Woman in National Costume* (Cat. 153) and in *Double*, the two works which have had so much influence on young contemporary painters, his form is close to what we find in the "papiers déchirés" of Arp. The *Guardian Angel* (Cat. 149) painted in 1939 also reminds one of Arp; but in these works Arp had naturally become Klee. Only Picasso, in the rare cases which Klee drew inspiration from him, did not become Klee.

EGYPTIAN WOMAN. 1940. *Felix Klee Collection, Berne.*

He was the only artist whom Klee did not succeed in absorbing.

The angels and saints—*Poor Angel, Stained-glass Saint* (Cat. 149)—have the splendour of a cathedral and are, as it were, forerunners of a barbaric Triumph of Death.

Suddenly a presentiment of the end seems to bring the artist back to Islam, which had always attracted him so greatly, and to Africa. Even the *Flower-girls* now have the eyes of spectres. It is useless to look for Mozart and Bach in the works of the last period; but there is Mussorgsky— the subdued funereal splendour of the *Catacombs*, one of the *tableaux* in the performance produced by Kandinsky at Dessau in 1928, in *Death and Fire* (Cat. 159), the famous tempera in the Rupf Collection. Its dense colours recall the last years of Titian, in whom —as a young man—Klee had refused to recognize a colourist of genius. Other works—such as the terrifying *Mask* in the Klee Foundation, are undisguisedly African.

His last work of all—a still life which is a gay harmony of greens, reds, oranges and blues, takes us back to the Klee of the happier years. Perhaps it is himself he has drawn in a corner of the picture in a life and death struggle with an angel whom he grips in two strong hands. But he is not only Jacob with the muscular arms; he is also the moon which gleams in the background in all its yellow fullness.

ROSINANTE'S GRANDSON. 1939. *Felix Klee Collection, Berne.*

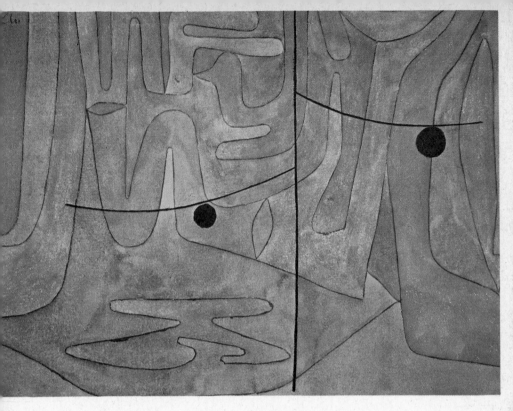

TWO FRUIT LANDSCAPE II. *Felix Klee Collection, Berne.*

The Last Days

In February 1940, only a few months before his death, Klee agreed to exhibit his works in the Kunsthaus in Zürich. Frau Carola Giedion-Welcker says that this great occasion was very badly received by the critics.

"When I saw Paul Klee for the last time", she says, "in May 1940 in his flat in Berne, I felt—in spite of his usual calm and impassiveness—that he was somewhat upset when he spoke of the latest display by the Swiss Press. The great exhibition of his last works in the Kunsthaus—the rich harvest of his last seven years in Switzerland—had been the occasion for numerous attacks and Philistine misunderstandings. This negative reaction seemed to be chiefly due to the fact that this 'painter of minute pictures' suddenly began to express himself in a monumental language of signs and runic characters.

"The reason why Klee was so annoyed by the notices in the press was that he thought they might have a dangerous effect on his life in Switzerland, for they seemed to be endangering the success of his request

NAVIGATIO MALA. 1939. *Klee-Stiftung, Berne.*

to the authorities of Berne for Swiss citizenship. This I learned only when, looking at the problem solely from the point of view of personal feelings, I argued that rude allusions to mental abnormality which were intended to flatter the public, could clearly not touch him in his inner self. He showed no interest in this side of the question, but remarked dryly that to be suspected of schizophrenia—both Joyce and Arp had gone through similar purgatory— undoubtedly did not encourage the authorities to grant permission to live in Switzerland. Klee was right. He was to die a few weeks later at Locarno-Muralto. The country of his mother's family, of his youth and his language—for he spoke pure Berne dialect even in Germany—was never to become officially his native land.

"Our conversation then passed on to more pleasant topics. He told me that he wanted to go south and rest, for the exhibition, with all its problems of organization, seemed to have tired him. In the course of our conversation, he was continually running in and out of the little kitchen for, as he remarked with a certain irony, women did not like cooking any more and most of the time he cooked for himself. Behind this irony there lay, in fact, a tragic explanation, to which typically he did not allude. In fact he could only take liquid food, specially prepared, and he had to watch carefully for the desire and opportunity to eat. But that was a subject he would not discuss. He accepted his illness with the same submissiveness to fate as Joyce accepted his half-blind state. He never complained and never devoted any particular attention to it. The best way of overcoming it was to integrate it through discipline into his work and daily life.

"In the course of his last years all his energies were directed towards completing and perfecting his vast œuvre. The progress of his illness does not seem to have diminished his productivity, but on the contrary to have stimulated him. His subconscious told him that he had to hurry, that time was pressing and death—as we can see from many of his pictures—was a constant and inexorable threat. What struggles, both physical and mental, lay behind this labour no one would ever know, for Klee was a man of great silences.

"That day I felt for the first time an intense desire to trace all the phases and all the varying expressions of this product of genius. I was attracted by the task of transmitting my own experience of an art born of so much silence and meditation—an art in which 'suffering is conquered by the spirit' (the title given by Klee to one of his earliest drawings) and in which

SCYLLA. 1938. *Klee-Stiftung, Berne.*

211

NEWLY LAID OUT GARDEN. 1937. *Private Collection, Berne.*

the artist's inner life was expressed through 'consoling symbols'. But in 1940 the climate of the times was not only a threat to the 'flowers of this sublime type of art' as the press impertinently said, but to the very reality in which they were rooted.

"It was only twelve years later that I was able to fulfil the desire which I had experienced in these troubled days of the war. The dominating aspects of my task seemed to me to be twofold: to make Klee's personality

emerge from the collective history of European art and, at the same time, to establish the relationship between his work and contemporary artistic life. One had to form links with the past in order to trace his deep roots in the culture of his own time and also to determine the influence upon him of a more distant past. For Klee was not an artist who placed the accent solely on the present. Like Arp he was steeped in memories. The influences which had affected him ranged from the

212

WITH GREEN STOCKINGS. 1939. *Felix Klee Collection, Berne.*

GROUP OF SEVEN. 1939. *Klee-Stiftung, Berne.*

214

FRATERNITY. 1939. *Klee-Stiftung, Berne*

Munich Jugendstil, the draughtsman, Gulbransson, and the grotesques of Christian Morgenstern to James Ensor and Goya, who has played a very special part through his fascination for modern artists."

Then there came that sharp turning-point—the awakening of Klee the painter. The beginning of something quite new stimulated by Robert Delaunay, who was a decisive influence not only on Klee but on many of his most gifted contemporaries, such as Macke and Marc. But what lay behind the metamorphosis which made a painter of a draughtsman, was not only the flower of French culture—there was also Nature: Klee's experience of colour in Africa. The phrase jotted in his Diary at Kairouan on 16th April, 1914, bears witness: "I and colour are one . . . I am a painter."

"After this direct experience of colour", Carola Giedion-Welcker continues, "Klee's world is no longer grotesque but mystical—an intellectual trend which affected both Germany and France in the twenties and found expression not only in painting but also in poetry. It was a phenomenon common to Europe; one to which Klee's art contributed its own vital

FURNISHED ARCTIC. 1935. *Calerie Rosengart, Lucerne.*

216

force. His inner life was such that the spirit of the times struck root there. It is not only in his writings and in his Diary that we find this new world but above all in the transparency of his painting, in his misty sublimation, which embraces all space. Here we find an entirely new mode of expression in the colour such as Robert Delaunay had introduced in 'Le cubisme orphique'. But Klee laid more stress on spiritual poetry and often linked the mystical element with an element of burlesque, comparable to the *Galgenlieder* of Morgenstern or the *Vie mystique et burlesque du Frère Matorel* of Max Jacob.

"The Bauhaus period, which begins in 1921, produces a kind of counterpoint. For ten years it brings Klee and Kandinsky together again. This is the period of theoretical reflection and study in the course of which he produced the *Pädagogisches Skizzenbuch*. More and more it appears that Klee's theoretical writings are, along with Kandinsky's, among the most instructive on modern art. Klee, like Albrecht Dürer, is a thinker and a seeker. What interest him are proportions, formulae and laws; in that he is the opposite of Picasso, as Dürer is of Grunewald. Of particular interest is his anticipation of the atmosphere of Egypt, his experience of it and the way in which he transformed it—all of which happened at the end of the Bauhaus period. Behind his proportional tensions and colour relations there flowers a new world of images. The composition, the structure, the rhythm, the coloured light, combine

217

EXOTIC TEMPLE GIRL. 1939. *Klee-Stiftung, Berne.*

218

ANOTHER CAMEL! 1939. *F. C. Schang Collection, New York.*

GREEN ON GREEN. 1938. *Dr. Hans Meyer-Benteli, Berne.*

to arouse a new feeling of space, to bring about a radical transformation of perspective into a completely new 'ubiquity'. Pictures like *Highway and Byways* are the most significant results of the Egyptian period and are among the finest treasures of contemporary art.

"The Klee exhibition in Zürich in 1940, in which the monumental images glowed like the characters of a Runic language revealed a style of drawing which was linear, black, thick —like great wooden beams—set on a coloured background; there was none of the transparency of twenty years before. The exhibition was a brilliant display of Klee's late style.

"It was during this exhibition that I understood that a new symbolical language had come to its maturity in these large-scale works, and that they

CALIGULA. 1936.
Felix Klee Collection, Berne.

A NEW ORDER—BUT ORDER. 1939. *Klee-Stiftung, Berne.*

were, perhaps, Klee's most important and most original contribution to European art of the twentieth century. There his philosophical mind could reveal itself in visible signs, conceived with the utmost simplicity and embracing both the present and the most remote past. Pictures like *Insula Dulcamara*, that fabulous island, which had haunted him since 1913, or the great picture *Project*, are new worlds, from both the optical and the intellectual point of view. These works bring his life and his work to a close in the grand manner. For Klee, as he said in 1919, art was not there to reproduce the visible but to render visible what lay hidden beyond the visual world. He remained faithful to this doctrine and brought its deep meaning to fruition until, after passing through many intermediary stages, he achieved in his pictorial world its last, essential beauty.''

VALKYRIE. 1940. *Klee-Stiftung, Berne.*

TREE IN THE TOWN. 1939. *Felix Klee Collection, Berne.*

224

EVENING IN THE SUBURBS. 1940. *Felix Klee Collection, Berne.*

'The Heart of Creation'

On 10th May, a few days after Carola Giedion-Welcker's visit, Klee felt the end to be near and was accompanied by his wife to a nursing home at Orselina near Locarno. A few months previously his old father had died and Klee had said to Lily: "You will see that I won't survive him long." From day to day his condition became worse. On 8th June the invalid was urgently transferred to a nursing home in Muralto-Locarno. Paralysis was approaching the heart. In order not to upset him no one talked of the war and they kept from him both the German offensive and the fall of Paris. He died on the morning of 29th June. He was cremated in Lugano on 1st July. On 4th July, a memorial service was attended by his wife and some friends including Hermann Rupf, Rolf Bürgi and Georg Schmidt, the keeper of the Basle Museum. His son was not present. He had seen his father for the last time at the end of the summer and had had a long talk with him about Sicily, from which he had just come back with his wife. Now he was mobilized somewhere in Germany. After the pastor, it was Georg Schmidt who spoke:

"Amidst the uproar of death", he said "the most silent and the most exceptional of modern artists has silently died. For long those who were close to him had trembled for that precious life. For in the last year of an exceptionally productive life a new harvest had come to maturity and seemed to foreshadow something completely new. Those who watched the drying up of the sap in the roots of his being could see in the more vigorous

225

tonalities of his later works a kind of triumph of creative will over matter and sought, therefore, to discover in the fruits of his maturity the first signs of a new flowering. Now we must lament a double loss—our human contact without friend and the promise of the unripened fruit.

"I have seen Klee's last works. However painful it may be for us to hear it, they do not contain any of the buds of a fresh spring. They are the finale of a life which knew its end to be near. We must admit even more precisely, truthfully, and painfully, that they are a variation on the theme:

Full Stop. Thus, to the end of his life, Klee in his works remained in harmony with the law of his being. The pride of triumphing over death for a few days, with a few works, has no place in that patient, submissive life.

"Klee's last works are not only more sombre in tonality—it seems as if in them the smile which played round his mouth and which we find in so many of his pictures has died away. It is the harshest possible symbols of inevitability, which multiply there, like the long-prepared finale of a symphony.

"Now Klee has lived through man's ultimate experience; but he had lived

THE SNAKE GODDESS AND HER ENEMY. 1940. *Private Collection, Berne.*

226

SPECTACLES IN A TANTRUM. 1938. *Klee-Stiftung, Berne.*

A CHILD'S GAME. 1939. *Felix Klee Collection, Berne.*

through many others—all those permitted to human beings, whether internal or external, in the language of tangible forms, of tangible, legible symbols. All of them! Everything external and visible; everything internal and invisible; all organized creatures, from man to the lowest orders of animal or vegetable existence; the totality of inorganic objects which man has made for his use; those which nature has formed by chance; those which are waiting to be integrated into life's evolutionary cycle.

"We would require a formidable catalogue of the possible phenomena

WANTS TO GO ABOARD. 1939. *Felix Klee Collection, Berne.*

in the human, animal and vegetable worlds, if we were to calculate what Klee knew and transmitted to us—and always his knowledge concerned the inner *raison d'être* of things, their essential quality, not their mere appearance. Suppose we attempt to assess what Klee knew and told us of the objects man uses—let us take those we know best, a house, our means of transport on earth, on water or in the air, then we will see on what affectionate terms he was with all objects familiar to man. Similarly we could list all the phenomena of our earth and its landscape—the totality of meteorological phenomena of the days and years; soon we should be obliged to tear ourselves away from this earth and, leaving it far behind us, launch out into the realm of the stars.

"It was in intermediary zones that Klee found his true climate: the intermediary state between night and day; between things constructed and those which grow naturally (for which Klee's symbol is the garden); the intermediary zone where the inorganic mutates into the organic, from plant to animal, from animal to human being. This series of gradations Klee did not look upon as a progression—for him it was a path which led as straight and as naturally in one direction as in the other. Klee did not measure reality with the petty scale of human cares, desires or needs; he gave himself to reality in all its forms. He abandons himself to it without restriction and with the utmost confidence, the deepest love for everything that exists, or could exist. For Klee, reality does not stop at the world of visible and tangible objects. It embraces the whole living world, the world which includes all organized beings and inorganized things, the active forces of formation, mutation and destruction.

"Perhaps it is in the field of specifically human psychology that Klee's

THROUGH POSEIDON. 1940. *Curt Valentin Collection, New York.*

ANTIQUE FIGURE. 1940. *Klee-Stiftung, Berne*.

art is richest. It is an art which knows anguish and turbulence, hate and love, gravity and frivolity, irony and faith. It knows arrogance and humility, melancholy and gaiety; it knows all possible human states in all their gradations. It knows good and bad spirits, germination and decomposition, flowering and decay. It knows all the intermediary phases between life and death. It knows life because it knows death. Klee is always ready for any adventure in the visible and invisible world.

"There is no other artist of our time who comes so close to whatever is living and formed, that is to say to reality, as Paul Klee, who was the most silent, the most refined, the most tender artist of our times.

"It is only if we are capable of distinguishing between *experience* of reality and objective representation—that is to say between realist thought and naturalist representation—that we shall understand that Klee is one of the greatest spirits in the domain of a reality which has been both experienced and artistically shaped—that he is the greatest realist of our times."

In September 1942, the urn containing the artist's ashes was taken to the Schlosshalde Cemetery in Berne. On Klee's grave is inscribed an extract from his Diary:

"I cannot be grasped in this world, for I am as much at home with the dead as with those yet unborn— a little nearer to the heart of creation than is normal but still too far away."

232

WITH THE TWO LOST ONES. 1938. *R. Doetsch-Benziger Collection, Basle.*

BIEDERMEIER-FRAULEIN. 1940. *Felix Klee Collection, Berne.*

HE ROWS DESPAIRINGLY. 1940. *Klee-Stiftung, Berne.*

An Unorthodox Saint

Klee gave to painting an unexplored world, whose frontiers—before his time—had been crossed only by poetry, music and mathematics. Admittedly Kandinsky also opened up a new world to the arts and Mondrian has brought us his absolute reality. But if the latter's 'truth' is too objective, the former's is too individual. Kandinsky rarely allows us to enter his world and we still have no real desire to enter Mondrian's. It is from the outside that we admire both Mondrian's solar universe and the more human stellar microcosm of Kandinsky.

Certain philosophers maintain that Klee's world is poetical but absurd—as it would indeed be did the artist not succeed in convincing us of its existence. If he failed to do so it would not even be poetic. Klee's paintings reveal an area of intuitive knowledge where the absurd has its own rigorous logic and therefore ceases to be absurd. Without using drugs, without opium, without mescalin, the artist, by virtue of the peculiar power and constitution

POOR ANGEL. 1939. *Private Collection, Berne.*

of his genius, attains to truth—an absolute truth, which is not, however, that of science. For if art replaced science and renounced intuition, it would inevitably find itself crippled in its revelationary function. Einstein, who, like Klee, was possessed by 'delirium mathematicum' was of the same opinion.

Klee's world is, if you like, a primitive one—a world of caves, but of stellar caves, which open up a new

GROUP WITH MAN RUNNING AWAY AND HURLING INSULTS. 1940. *Klee-Stiftung, Berne.*

cycle of civilization on a more advanced planet. Some day, perhaps, another great artist will reveal a vaster area of knowledge but he will not be able to overshadow Klee's work, because for Klee each technical problem was a problem of style. However subtle and refined it may be, his technique is never an end in itself. It is the very essence of the painting. Even his humour, which to begin with was the mainspring of his art, in the years of maturity is only the spark from which his work is born.

The question remains whether the world of Klee's art always corresponds to what the artist attempted to define in his writings—including the thousands of pages of his unpublished papers on the doctrine of style and of projection into space, on regular forms, on the square, the circle, the ellipse, the parabola, the hyperbole and so on. It is a question which cannot be answered without a certain embarrassment for it seems that the two universes—the one he conceived mentally and the one he created plastically—meet only like two stars in the sky; that is to say, never to the point of fusion. In short, fortunately for us, Klee the artist never realizes more than a tiny portion of the ambitions of Klee the thinker. Had he realized them all, he would inevitably have become subject to the limitations of science, which he rightly rejected. His artist's nature always saved him from his danger. If we admire him when he succeeds as a thinker he is still more precious to us when his thought, without any hint of pre-meditation, acquires form by intuitive use of the most direct methods—not only when it expresses itself in simple symbols familiar to our Western sensibilities, as when he meditates on the growth of a tree or on man with the eternal tear in his eyes, but also in the 'magic squares' and the still more magical Egyptian landscapes. Perhaps he is then unwittingly much nearer to the heart of creation, that supreme goal of the artist.

It would be a mistake to judge Klee the artist entirely from the point of view of Klee the theoretician. It would in any case, as Grohmann recognizes, be an impossible task. Klee himself, when judging his work, used to amuse himself by giving marks. Sometimes he went so far as to mark his water colours with the letters S.C., which stood for *Sonder-Classe*—special category. But he always judged his own work from the point of view of the artist and not the philosopher.

When faced with the exceptional richness of Klee's *imagerie*, one might perhaps say that it is in fact a reflection of the cosmic fervour of his thought. But there is something else there— that humour which we rarely find in his theoretical writings. There is humour even in the gloomy pictures of his last days. The still life, which was the last of his works, is by way of being the triumph of humour over the preceding paintings. Klee's humour can only be reconciled with the mysticism of Klee the thinker in the same way as we justify the unorthodox ways of certain saints. The difficulty is to decide when he is being the more

ECCE. 1940. *Felix Klee Collection, Berne.*

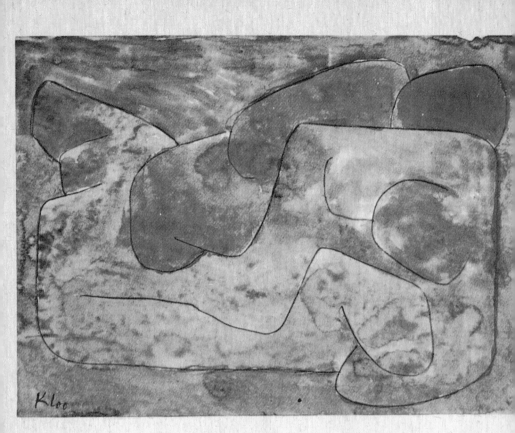

NAKED ON THE BED. 1939. *Felix Klee Collection, Berne.*

unorthodox—when he is theorizing
mystically or when he turns back to
gaze at the full moon and the slender
pine tree or to listen to the canary's
mechanical song. But the poet in him
must not have all our affection. Along-
side the poet there is the painter who,
even when he is joking, reveals to the
young painters the real problems of
art and fires the first unerring arrow.
This aspect of him as the apostle of
contemporary painting, in which he has

an undisputed primacy, is no less
worthy of our affection and gratitude.

What does surprise us is his obstin-
ate search for impastos, for colours,
for materials, which certainly allowed
him to give expression to his passion for
alchemy (he was a twentieth-century
wizard) and to attain certain wonderful effects; but they were not always
indispensable. His conviction that each
work demands its own materials
appears excessive—particularly if we

consider the fact that, in spite of all his alchemy, his colours are always of the simplest, and most common. What his mania did was to reveal to him that elementary poetry in an artist's materials which the Cubists had casually discovered. A fragment of sackcloth with the right patch of colour can move our feelings as much as a canvas painted in the grand style —perhaps even more, because of that thirst for novelty, for surprise, which is in each one of us.

Some people—including his son Felix—consider that his illness was due to slow poisoning brought on by the toxic substances in the colours which he handled so haphazardly.

Will Grohmann has rightly said that one could write ten different books on Klee. If one were to write another dealing only with his work, it would be limited to his first definition of art —the definition he got from Oscar Wilde: symbols and space. (From his early works Klee shows a profound intuitive understanding for space.) One could, on the other hand, study his colour alone; then one would discover that the artist put the critics on to a false trail with that famous phrase at Kairouan. For they ignore all his preceding work, except for the drawings and etchings. Yet Klee was a born colourist, as is clear from his youthful paintings. In 1913

GLANCE. 1940. *Klee-Stiftung, Berne.*

he was no less great as a colourist than in 1914 after the journey to Tunis. In Kairouan, if you like, he celebrated his wedding with colour; but like his wedding with Lily it had been preceded by long years of passionate love. His hesitation was due solely to his fight against the age in which he lived, which attempted to impose its own taste and its own attitude to art; but in the end it was he who imposed his own genius and his own taste.

We can never exhaust Klee's work. It yields up its secrets only to the extent that we delve into it more and more deeply. For that we must live with it for a long time. We wander about in it at random and little by little the magic takes effect. We feel ourselves insensibly caught in the net of this enchanted universe, which is so close to our own and which pro-vides it with a mysterious second meaning.

He is a painter which we must constantly have to hand if we wish to learn to know plants, water and the wind, to lose ourselves in the maze of enchanted roads leading to no-where, in the depths of the under-growth where strange music plays. Some of his works are set and immov-able as if petrified. Theirs is an embalmed beauty. Others belong to all time, for they contain such a range of power that they can respond to all mankind's innumerable aspirations; as it changes they also change. As fragile and perishable as those who seek refuge in them and the respite of a moment, they bear the promise that what in man is most delicate, most free, and most threatened—his dreams —may yet survive.

POEM IN PICTURE SCRIPT. 1939. *Felix Klee* **Collection, Berne.**

Biographical Notes

SAILING SHIPS MOVING GENTLY. 1927. *Private Collection, Berne.*

KLEE—Biographical Notes.

1879   18th December. Birth of Paul Klee at Münchenbucksee near Berne.
        His father, who is music master at the training school for teachers at
        Berne-Hofwyl, is German; his mother Swiss.
1880   The Klee family—father and mother, Paul and his sister Mathilde—born
        in 1876—settles in Berne.
1880   Birth of Franz Marc, Ernst Ludwig Kirchner and Hermann Haller.
1881   Birth of Picasso.
1882   Birth of Braque.
1884   Birth of Karl Schmidt-Rottluf.
1885   Birth of Delaunay.
1886–1898 Klee attends primary school and the Berne Gymnasium. Takes his
        Matura.
        At the age of seven he learns to play the violin.
        At the age of ten, he sees his first opera—*il Trovatore*.
1887   Birth of August Macke.
1896   The two reviews *Jugend* and *Simplizissimus* begin to appear in Munich;

245

THE PARK AT ABIEN. 1939 *Felix Klee Collection, Berne.*

they will spread the *Jugendstil* and publish drawings by Th. Heine, Olaf Gulbransson and others, which will influence Klee.

Kandinsky, born in Moscow in 1886, and Javlensky, born at Suslovo in 1864, come to Munich and meet at Anton Azbé's school of painting.

1898   In October, Klee goes to Munich and enters Knirr's school of art. He once more meets the sculptor Hermann Haller, whom he had known since 1886.

1899   In the autumn he meets the pianist Lily Stumpf (born 1876), daughter of a Munich doctor; she will become his wife in 1906.

1900   In October Klee enrolls at the Munich Academy and joins Franz Stuck's

POMONA. 1938. *Klee-Stiftung, Berne.*

studio; Kandinsky is also studying there. But the two men do not meet. Klee takes courses on the history of art, studies anatomy, practises modelling and takes his first steps in the technique of etching.

1901 He leaves the Academy and goes on a journey to Italy with Hermann Haller. He visits Milan (22nd October), Genoa, Leghorn, Pisa, Rome (27th October–23rd March 1902).

1902 Naples (23rd March–6th April), Rome (7th–13th April), Florence (15th April–2nd May). He returns to Berne where he stays until 1906.

1902 Kandinsky opens an art school in Munich.

247

1903   In Berlin Karl Scheffler and Casar Flaischlen found the review *Kunst und Künstler*, to which Klee will later submit some of his drawings.

1903–1905   Klee produces his first ten etchings. He reads greatly and goes frequently to the theatre, to the opera and to concerts. He plays a great deal of music himself and is violinist in the Berne municipal orchestra.

1904   During a trip to Munich he studies the work of Beardsley, Blake and Goya in the Kupferstichkabinet.

1905   Klee produces his first "sous-verres". He visits Paris along with his Swiss friends Hans Bloesch and Louis Moilliet (31st May–13th June). Visits the Louvre and the Musée du Luxembourg. Is particularly interested in Leonardo da Vinci, Goya, Velasquez, Tintoretto, Watteau, Chardin, Puvis de Chavannes, Manet, Monet, and Renoir. No mention in his diary of the new painters of the day—Matisse, Picasso, etc.
In Paris the Fauves exhibit in the Salon d'Automne.
In Dresden the Expressionist painters—Kirchner, Heckel, Schmidt-Rotluff —found *Die Brücke*.

1906   Klee exhibits six etchings at the Sezession in Munich.
From 8th to 16th April he is in Berlin with Bloesch. At the National Galerie he sees the Centenary Exhibition and is particularly interested in Feuerbach, Marées, Leibl, Trübner, Menzel and Liebermann. On the way home he breaks his journey at Kassel to admire the Rembrandts in the Museum.
At Karlsruhe he is "terrified" by Grünewald's *Crucifixion*.
15th September—marriage to Lily Stumpf.
In October he settles in Munich. In order to support them his wife teaches music while he looks after the house.
Offers some drawings to *Simplizissimus*; they are not accepted.
Kandinsky goes to Paris for a year.

1907   Klee submits etchings and "sous-verres" to Karl Scheffler who refuses to publish them in *Kunst und Künstler*.
Three "sous-verres" which he submits to the jury of the Munich Sezession are also rejected.
He sees some Impressionist paintings in a Munich gallery; he particularly admires Manet.
He sees a large collection of Toulouse-Lautrec; he is most interested by the drawings and lithographs.
His Swiss friend Ernst Sonderegger introduces him to the work of Ensor and Daumier.
30th November—birth of his only child, Felix.

1908   Sonderegger makes him read the letters of Van Gogh; shortly after he sees two very important exhibitions of his work in the Munich galleries.
The *Bund Zeichnender Künstler*, an association of artists interested in drawing, refuses to make him a member.

The Debschltz School employs him for some months to supervise its evening classes for drawing from the nude.

The Munich Sezession, to which he sends six of his sous-verres, accepts only three.

He offers the etching *Hero with a Wing* to Franz Biel for the review *Hyperion*. It is never published.

He sends six drawings to the Berlin Sezession, which exhibits them in its black and white Salon.

Cubism born in Paris.

1909 He describes an exhibition by Hans von Marées at the Munich Sezession as "an event".

He sees eight pictures by Cézanne at the Sezession and discovers in him the master *par excellence* who teaches him much more than Van Gogh.

On Franz Biel's advice he submits some drawings to Meier-Graefe, who is reticent about them. Some of these drawings, which Biel had wanted to publish in *Hyperion* are finally sent back to him without having been published.

He plans to illustrate Voltaire's *Candide*.

The Berlin Sezession exhibits some of his work.

Kandinsky founds the *Neue Künstlervereinigung* in Munich along with Javlensky, Marc, Kubin and others.

The first Futurist Manifesto appears in Milan and Paris.

1910 Klee exhibits fifty-six of his works from the years 1907–1910 at the Berne Museum, at the Zurich Kunsthaus and in a gallery in Winterthur.

One of his drawings is acquired by Alfred Kubin (born 1877).

Kandinsky writes *Concerning the Spiritual Element in Art* and paints his first abstract composition.

In Berlin, Herwarth Walden (born 1878) founds the avant-garde *Der Sturm*.

The Manifesto of Futurist Painters (Carrà, Boccioni, Balla, Severini and Russolo) appears in Milan.

1911 The exhibition organized in Berne the year before is shown in Basle.

The critic Wilhelm Michel submits some of Klee's drawings to the editor of the review *Kunst und Dekoration*, who refuses to publish them, and to the Munich art dealer, Thannhauser, who agrees to exhibit thirty of them in the corridor of his gallery.

Klee produces his illustrations to *Candide*.

He meets August Macke at the house of Louis Moilliet in Switzerland.

He is one of the founder-members of *Sema*—an association of artists which includes, among others, Kubin, Caspar and Scharff.

He meets Kandinsky, Franz Marc, Heinrich Campendonck, Marianne von Werefkin, Gabriela Münter and Hans Arp.

Kandinsky, Marc, Kubin and Gabriela Münter leave the *Neue Künstler-vereinigung*. The first two work on a book which will appear in 1912 under the title of *Der Blaue Reiter*; in December they organize an important exhibition with the same title at Thannhauser's. It brings together forty-three pictures by Henri Rousseau, Robert Delaunay, Kandinsky, Marc, Macke, Campendonck, etc. Klee is most impressed by Delaunay, who exhibits five works, among them *Saint-Séverin* (1909) and *La Ville* (1911).

1912   Klee participates in the second exhibition of the *Blaue Reiter* group, which is held in the Goltz Gallery and is composed entirely of drawings and etchings.

From 2nd to 18th April he visits Paris, goes to see Delaunay and Le Fauconnier and visits the galleries of Wilhelm Uhde where he finds works by Henri Rousseau, Braque and Picasso, of Kahnweiler (Derain, Vlaminch and Picasso), of Bernheim-Jeune (Matisse) and others. Delaunay sends him an article which he translates for *Der Sturm*. It is published in the number for January 1913, under the title of *On Light*.

Klee meets Karl Wolfskehl, the friend of Stefan George.

In the Thannhauser Gallery, he admires an exhibition of Italian futurists—Carrà, Boccioni, Severini and Russolo—arranged by Herwarth Walden, who in that same year opens the Sturm Gallery in Berlin.

Kandinsky publishes his book on *Spirituality in Art*.

1913   Arp puts Klee into contact with the writer Otto Flake, with a view to publishing his illustrations for *Candide* in the *Weisse Blätter*. Klee exhibits in the Sturm Gallery and takes part in the same gallery in the first German Salon d'Automne, which presents a wide survey of modern European art with 360 pictures.

Kandinsky publishes his autobiographical essay *Rückblicke* in *Der Sturm*.

1914   Klee is one of the founders of the New Munich Sezession—a group instigated by the critic Wilhelm Hausenstein; Marc and Kandinsky do not take part.

Journey to Tunisia in the company of Moilliet and Macke. 3rd–6th April: Munich, Berne, Geneva, Lyons, Marseilles. 7th April: arrival in Tunis—visits to Saint-Germain, Sidi-bou-Said, Carthage, Hamammet and Kairuan. 19th April: leaves Tunis. Returns by way of Palermo, Naples, Rome, Milan, Munich, which he reaches on 25th April. This journey is of the utmost importance for Klee's development. It brings him the revelation of colour; he confirms his conviction that he is a painter.

1st August—outbreak of war.

Marc, Macke and Campendonck are mobilized. Kandinsky, Javlensky, Marianne von Werefkin and Gabriele Münter leave Germany. Klee stays on in Munich.

16th August—Macke killed in Champagne.

PRECIPICE IN THE ALPS. 1938. *Felix Klee Collection, Berne.*

1915 Klee receives a visit from Rilke. In the course of the summer he goes to Switzerland with the permission of the German military authorities.
He begins modelling and colouring statuettes.
1916 Franz Marc killed at Verdun.

11th March—Klee mobilized in the *Landsturm*. He is sent first to Landshut and then to Munich (end of July–August), then to Schleissheim where he is stationed in an air-force depot. He works as a painter and accompanies convoys—to Cologne and Saint-Quentin.

The first demonstrations of the Dada group, founded by Hans Arp, the Roumanian poet, Tristan Tzara and the German writers, Hugo Ball and Richard Hüsenbeck, take place in the Cabaret Voltaire in Zürich.

1917   Klee is still stationed at Schleissheim; he accompanies a convoy to Nordholz near Cuxhaven. On his way back he stops at Berlin and visits Herwarth Walden and the collector Bernard Koehler.

16th January—he is transferred to Gersthofen near Augsburg, where he is employed as pay clerk.

He exhibits at the *Sturm* Gallery and sells several of his works.

The poet Theodor Däubler, devotes a flattering article to him in the *Berliner Börsencourier*.

In Leyden, Theo van Doesburg founds *De Stijl*, the review of *Neo-Plasticism*, along with Piet Mondrian, Vilmos Huszar, Georges Vantongerloo and others.

1918   Klee remains at Gersthofen until after the armistice. Towards Christmas he is demobilized and returns to his family in Munich.

In Berlin, Walden publishes the *Sturm-Bilderbuch* made up of drawings from *Der Sturm*, including fifteen drawings by Klee.

Kandinsky becomes professor at the Academy of Art in Moscow.

1919   In Munich Klee rents a large studio in the Suresnes Palace. Two painters, Willi Baumeister and Oskar Schlemmer, try to have him taken on as professor at the Stuttgart Academy; but he is turned down.

He signs a contract with the picture dealer Goltz. Kahnweiler begins to buy his pictures.

The *Kestnerbuch*, which appears in Hanover and to which Thomas Mann, Daubler, Döblin, Worringer, Heckel, Schwitters and Feininger contribute, publishes a lithograph by Klee.

The architect, Walter Gropius (born 1883) founds the Bauhaus in Weimar. Lyonel Feininger (born 1871) and Johannes Itten (born 1888), both painters, and the sculptor Gerhard Marcks (born 1889) and other representatives of advanced art and architecture become professors there.

1920   Klee has a big exhibition in Munich at Goltz's gallery with 362 works. The Berlin review *Tribüne der Kunst und Zeit*, edited by Kasimir Edschmid publishes *Creative Confession*, which Klee began to write in 1918.

His illustrations to *Candide*, which date from 1911, are published by Kurt Wolff in Munich.

Another work illustrated by him—Curt Corrinth's *Potsdamer Platz*—is published by Georg Müller in Munich.

Hans von Wedderkop and Leopold Zahn each devote a monograph to him. On 25th November he is invited to become a professor at the Bauhaus.

1921   Klee leaves Munich for Weimar.

At the Bauhaus he begins with *Formmeister* (master of form) in a glass workshop then in the weaving school. Later he also teaches painting.

Wilhelm Hausenstein publishes his monograph *Kairuan, or The History of the Painter Klee and the Art of our Time.*

Death of Klee's mother.

Theo von Doesburg lectures at the Bauhaus and spreads the ideas of Neo-Plasticism.

Oskar Schlemmer becomes a professor at the Bauhaus.

In Moscow Kandinsky founds the All-Russian Academy of Arts and Sciences.

1922   Klee takes part in exhibitions at Wiesbaden and Berlin.

Kandinsky, who returned to Germany towards the end of 1921, also becomes a professor at the Bauhaus.

1923   Klee publishes *Ways of Studying Nature* in the publication *Staatliches Bauhaus in Weimar 1919–1923.*

Klee passes the summer on the island of Baltrum in the North Sea. In Hanover he visits Kurt Schwitters and El Lissitsky.

He exhibits in the Kronprinzenpalast in Berlin.

Itten leaves the Bauhaus. He is replaced by Moholy-Nagy.

1924   First Klee exhibition in the United States, in New York.

Foundation in Weimar of the *Blauen Vier* group: Kandinsky, Klee, Feininger and Javlensky.

Léon-Paul Fargue visits Klee in Weimar.

Voyage to Sicily—Taormina, Mazzaro, Syracuse, Gela.

Klee gives a lecture in Jena *On Modern Art*; it is not published until 1945.

On 26th December the Bauhaus is compelled to shut down in Weimar.

In Paris André Breton publishes the first Surrealist manifesto.

1925   In April the teachers and pupils of the Bauhaus settle in Dessau.

Klee publishes his *Pedagogical Sketches* in the series Bauhaus-Bücher.

He has a second large exhibition of 214 works in Goltz's gallery.

He takes part in the first exhibition of Surrealist painters, which is held in Paris in the Galerie Pierre, along with Arp, de Chirico, Max Ernst, Mirò, Picasso and others.

He also has his first one man exhibition in Paris in the Galerie Vavin-Raspail.

Piet Mondrian and Oskar Schlemmer publish books in the *Bauhaus-Bücher* —the first *The New Composition* and the second on *The Stage and the Bauhaus.*

1926   Klee goes to Italy—Elba, Pisa, Florence and Ravenna.

Kandinsky publishes *Point, Line and Surface* in the Bauhaus.

The new Bauhaus building by Gropius in Dessau is opened.

Publication of the first number of the *Bauhaus* review, which continues until 1932.

1927 Klee stays on Porquerolles and in Corsica. On his way back he visits Avignon.

Casimir Malevitch, the originator of *Suprématisme*, publishes *The World of Non-Representation* in the *Bauhaus-Bücher*.

1928 Klee visits Brittany and Belle-Isle.

The *Kleegesellschaft* founded by the collector, Otto Rahlfs, of Brunswick, offers him a trip to Egypt. He leaves on 17th December and does not return until 17th January 1929. Itinerary—Genoa, Alexandria, Cairo, Gizeh, Luxor, Karnak, the Valley of the Kings, Thebes, Aswan, Elephant Island, Syracuse, Dessau.

In the *Bauhaus* review he publishes *Exact Experiments in the Realm of Art.*

Gropius and Moholy-Nagy leave the Bauhaus. The Swiss architect, Hannes Meyer, becomes the new director.

1929 Klee makes a journey to the South of France—Carcassonne, Bayonne, the Gulf of Gascony—with an excursion to San Sebastian and Pamplona.

For his fiftieth birthday the Flechtheim Gallery in Berlin organizes a large exhibition of his works.

Exhibition in the Galerie Bernheim Jeune in Paris.

Will Grohmann publishes a monograph in the *Cahiers d'Art* in Paris.

Oskar Schlemmer leaves the Bauhaus.

1930 Klee spends some time in the Engadine and at Viareggio.

Another exhibition in Flechtheim's gallery.

Exhibition in the Museum of Modern Art, New York.

He becomes a member of the committee and jury of the *Deutcher Künstlerbund.*

The architect Mies van de Rohe, succeeds Hannes Meyer as director of the Bauhaus.

1931 On 1st April Klee terminates his contract with the Bauhaus and accepts a chair offered to him by the Düsseldorf Academy. He finds Campendonck there. Among the other professors there is Matisse's former pupil, Oskar Moll, as well as the sculptors Alexander Zschokke and Ewald Mataré.

Klee makes a second journey to Sicily—Syracuse, Ragusa, Agrigento, Palermo and Monreale.

1932 Journey to Switzerland and Italy (Venice).

Klee sees an exhibition of Picasso at the Kunsthaus, Zürich. Under pressure from the Nazis the Bauhaus leaves Dessau and settles in Berlin (Freies Bauhaus).

1933 Journey to the Midi—Saint Raphael, Hyères, Port-Cros.

Klee is violently attacked by the Nazis and is finally dismissed.

About Christmas time he leaves Germany and settles permanently in

HE GOES PAST—SUSPICIOUSLY. 1939. *Klee-Stiftung, Berne.*

Switzerland. He once more installs himself in Berne where his father and sister are still living.

Kandinsky also leaves Germany. Henceforth he will live at Neuilly-sur-Seine near Paris.

1934   First Klee exhibition in England at the Mayor Gallery, London.

Kahnweiler becomes Klee's dealer.

Grohmann publishes a collection of his drawings in Germany; the book is confiscated by the Nazis.

1935   Large retrospective exhibition in the Kunsthalle, Berne.

First symptom of the illness—sclerodermia—which will lead to his death five years later.

1936   His illness depresses him and he works little. He takes treatment at Tarasp and Montana without appreciable results.

Feininger leaves Germany and returns to the United States.

1937   Klee resumes his work.

Stay at Ancona where he visits the widow of Franz Marc.

Ernst Ludwig Kirchner, who lives near Davos, comes to see him as do Picasso and Braque.

He sees Kandinsky for the last time on the occasion of an exhibition of Kandinsky's work in the Kunsthalle, Berne.

The Nazis include seventeen works by Klee in the exhibition of "degenerate art"—at first in Munich and later in other German cities. They confiscate 102 of them from public collections and auction them.

1938   Klee is represented at the Bauhaus exhibition organized by the Museum of Modern Art, New York.

He exhibits in New York at the Buchholtz and Nierendorf Galleries and in Paris at Kahnweiler's and Carré's.

1939   Klee rests by a lake near Berne.

He visits the exhibition of masterpieces from the Prado at Geneva and greatly admires El Greco, Goya, Bosch and Breughel.

German troops invade Poland on 1st September. Felix Klee is called up.

1940   Large Klee exhibition in the Kunsthaus, Berne, of works dated 1935–1940.

Death of Klee's father.

On 10th May, Klee enters the Sanatorium at Orsolina near Locarno.

On 8th June, he is moved to the Sant' Agnese Clinic at Muralto-Locarno.

On 28th June he dies there of paralysis of the heart.

On 1st July he is cremated at Lugano.

On 4th July a funeral service is held in the Hôpital des Bourgeois, Berne.

1942   In September the urn containing Klee's ashes is interred in the Schlosshalde cemetery in Berne.

Catalogue
of Principal Works

1. Elfenau, Berne. 1897.

2. Zwei Männer, einander in höherer Stellung
vermutend, begegnen sich. 1903.

Die Schwester des Künstlers. 1903.

4. Komiker I. 1904.

5. Drohendes Haupt. 1905.

6. Lily Klee. 1905.

7. Gartenszene mit der Giesskanne. 1905.

1. Elfenau, Berne.   2. Two Men meet, each supposing the other to be of Higher Rank.
3. The Artist's Sister.   4. Comedian I.   5. Menacing Head.
6. Lily Klee.   7. Garden Scene with Watering-can.

8. Blumenmädchen mit kleinen
   Farbflecken. 1909.

9. Männlicher Kopf, jugendlich,
   mit blauen Augen. 1910.

10. Mutter und Kind 1913.

11. Ansicht von Saint-Germain. 1914.

12. Teppich der Erinnerung. 1914.

13. Motiv aus Hamammet. 1914.

14. Hommage à Picasso. 1914.

15. Städtische Darstellung. 19

8. Young Flower-girl with Stippling.   9. Head of young Man with blue Eyes.   10. Mother and Child.

11. View of Saint-Germain.   12. Carpet of Memory.

13. Motif from Hamammet.   14. Hommage à Picasso.   15. Representation of a City.

16. Der Niesen. 1915.

17. Kakendaemonisch. 1916.

18. Farbenwinkel. 1917

19. Composition mit Symbolen. 1917.

20. Mit dem gelben Halbmond und blauen Stern. 1917.

21. Ab ovo. 1917.

22. Fest auf dem Wasser. 1917.

16. The Niesen.   17. Kakendaemonisch.
18. Colour Corner.   19. Composition with Symbols.   20. With the yellow half Moon and blue Star.
21. Ab Ovo.   22. Festival on the Water.

23. Einsiedelei. 1918.   24. Mit dem Adler. 1918.

25. Dreitakt, mit der Drei. 1919.   26. Villa R. 1919.   27. Composition mit dem B. 1919

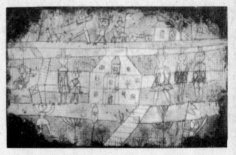

28. Abstrakt mit Vollmond. 1919.   29. Ankunft der Gaukler. 1920.

23. Hermitage.   24. With the Eagle.
25. Three-part Time.   26. Villa R.   27. Composition with the Letter B.
28. Abstract with full Moon.   29. Arrival of the Ballad Singers.

30. Bob. 1920.

31. Schulhaus. 1920.

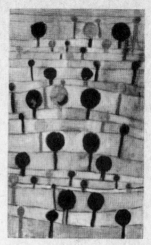

32. Rhythmische Baumlandschaft. 1920.

33. Zimmerperspektive mit
Einwohnern. 1921.

34. Hängende Früchte. 1921.

35. Keramisch - Erotisch - Religiös
(Die Gefässe der Aphrodite). 1921.

30. Bob.   31. School.   32. Rhythmical Landscape with Trees.
33. Perspective of a Room with Inmates.   34. Hanging Fruits.   35. Ceramic - Erotic - Religious
(The Vessels of Aphrodite).

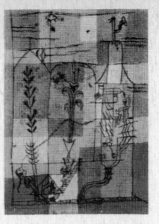

37. Hoffmanneske Märchenszene. 1921.

36. Gedenkblatt für Lieschen. 1921.

38. Die Heilige. 1921.

40. Die Zwitschermaschine. 1922.

39. Blütenantlitze. 1922.

41. Sterbende Pflanzen. 1922.

36. Souvenir for Lieschen.   37. Scene from a Hoffman-like Tale.   38. The Saint.
   39. Face of a Flower.   40. The Twittering Machine.   41. Dying Plants.

42. Drei Häuser. 1922.

43. Mystische Miniatüre. 1922.

4. Schwankendes Gleichgewicht.
1922.

45. Architektur (Gelb-violett
gestufte Kuben). 1923.

46. Bauchredner (Rufer im Moor).
1923.

47. Assyrisches Spiel. 1923.

48. Kampfszene aus der komischphantastischen
Oper " Der Seefahrer ". 1923.

42. Three Houses.   43. Mystical Miniature.
44. Unstable Equilibrium.   45. Architecture (Piled yellow and violet Cubes).   46. Ventriloquist - Man shouting in the Bog.
47. Assyrian Game.   48. Battle Scene from the comic-fantastic Opera " The Seafarer ".

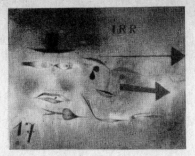

49. 17 IRR 1923.   50. Perspektive mit offener Türe. 1923.

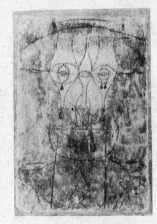

51. Eros. 1923.   52. Lomolarm. 1923.   53. Am Berg des Stieres. 1923.

54. Sonnen-und   Mondblumen.   1923.   55. Wattenmeer (Baltrum). 1923.

49. 17 (IRR) (Note: irr = lost, mad).   50. Perspective with open Door.
51. Eros.   52. The Weeping Man.   53. At the Mountain of the Bull.
            54. Sun and Moon Flowers.   55. Tideland at Baltrum.

56. Schauspielermaske. 1924.

57. Wasserpflanzenschriftbild. 1924.

58. Kleine Winterlandschaft mit dem
Skiläufer. 1924.

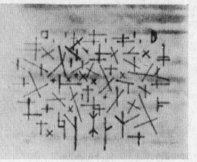

59. Zeichensammlung. 1924.

60. Felsen am Meer. 1924.

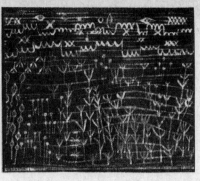

61. Gebirge im Winter. 1925.

56. Actor's Mask.   57. Script Picture - Water Plants.
58. Little Winter Landscape with Skier.   59. Collection of Signs.
60. Cliffs by the Sea.   61. Mountains in Winter.

62. Mystisch - Keramisch (in der Art eines Stillebens). 1925.

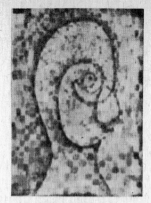

63. Kopfprofil. 1925.

64. Um den Fisch. 1926.

65. Hetäre auf ihrem Lager. 1926.

66. Abfahrt der Schiffe. 1927.

67. Variationen (progressives Motiv). 1927.

62. Mystic - Ceramic.   63. Profile.
64. Around the Fish.   65. Hetaera on her Couch.
66. The Ships depart.   67. Variations - Progressive Motif.

68. Zweihügel-Stadt. 1927.

69. Zeiten der Pflanzen. 1927.

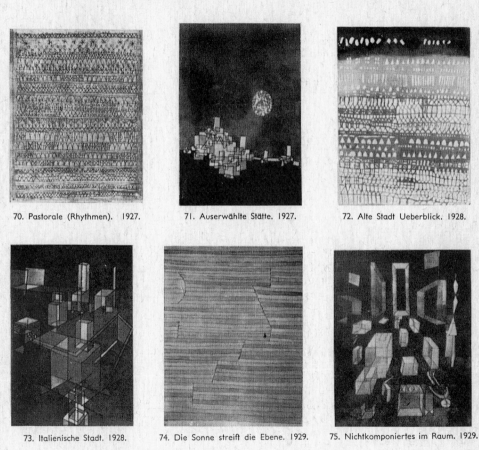

70. Pastorale (Rhythmen). 1927.

71. Auserwählte Stätte. 1927.

72. Alte Stadt Ueberblick. 1928.

73. Italienische Stadt. 1928.

74. Die Sonne streift die Ebene. 1929.

75. Nichtkomponiertes im Raum. 1929.

68. City on two Hills.   69. Times of the Plants.
70. Pastorale - Rhythms.   71. Chosen Site.   72. Old Town - Panorama.
73. Italian Town.   74. The Sun sweeps the Plain.   75. Uncomposed Objects in Space.

76. Ein Kreuzfahrer. 1929.   77. Hauptweg und Nebenwege. 1929.   78. Clown. 1929.

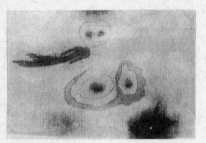

79. Irrende Seele. 1929.   80. Vor dem Schnee. 1929.

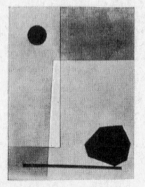

81. Nekropolis. 1929.   82. Gewagt wägend. 1930.   83. Zwillinge. 1930.

76. A Crusader.   77. Highway and Byways.   78. Clown.
79. Wandering Soul.   80. Before the Snow.
81. Necropolis.   82. Calmly daring.   83. Twins.

84. Pop und Lok im Kampf. 1930.

85. Physiognomien von Querschnitten. 1930.

86. Um sieben über Dächern. 1930.

87. Haus, aussen und innen. 1930.

88. Rhythmisches. 1930.

89. Winterbild. 1930.

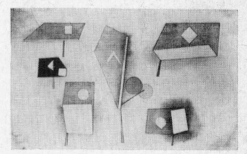

90. Sechs Arten. 1930.

84. Pop and Lok fighting.   85. Physiognomies of Cross-sections.
86. Seven o'clock above the Roofs.   87. Inside and Outside of a House.   88 Rhythmical.
89. Winter Picture.   90. Six Types.

271

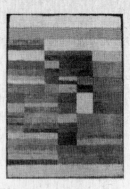

91. Segelnde Stadt. 1930.   92. Nekropolis. 1930.   93. Individualisierte Höhenmessung der Lagen. 1930.

94. Bäume im Oktober. 1931.   95. Ein Stich. 1931.

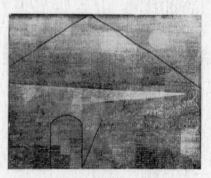

96. Schach. 1931.   97. Ad Parnassum. 1932.

91. Floating Town.   92. Necropolis.   93. Individualised Measurement of the Beds.
94. Trees in October.   95. A Stitch.
96. Check !   97. Ad Parnassum.

272

 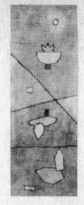 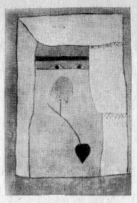

98. Tänzerin. 1932. 99. Pflanzen - analytisches. 1932. 100. Arabisches Lied. 1932.

101. Pflanzen Schriftbild. 1932. 102. Kleine Felsenstadt. 1932.

103. Kleiner blauer Teufel. 1933. 104. Der Künftige. 1933. 105. Frauenmaske. 1933.

98. Dancer. 99. Plants - analytic. 100. Arab Song.
101. Plant Script Picture. 102. Small Town among the Rocks.
103. Little blue Devil. 104. The Man of the Future. 105. Female Mask.

273

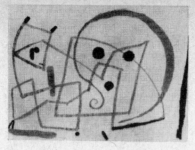

106. Dame und Tier. 1933.

107. Angst. 1934.

108. Botanisches Theater. 1934.

109. Blühendes. 1934.

110. Trauernd. 1934.

111. W-geweihtes Kind. 1935.

112. Dame Dämon. 1935.

106. Lady and Animal.   107. Fear.
108. Botanical Theatre.   109. Blossom.
110. Mourning.   111. Child consecrated to W (Woe).   112. Dame Demon.

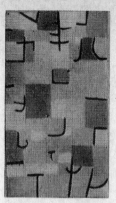

113. Zeichen auf dem Feld. 1935.   114. Betroffene Stadt. 1936.   115. Zeichen in Gelb. 1937.

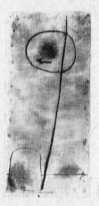

6. Labiler Wegweiser. 1937.   117. Ueberschach. 1937.   118. Ein Blick aus Aegypten. 1937.

119. Gedanken an Nachkommenschaft. 1937.   120. Harmonisierter Kampf. 1937.

113. Signs in the Field.   114. Stricken Town.   115. Yellow Signs.
116. Unstable Signpost.   117. Super-check !   118. A Glance from Egypt.
119. Thoughts on our Descendants.   120. Harmonised Struggle.

275

121. Garten im Orient. 1937.   122. Beginnende Kühle. 1937.   123. Revolution des Viaduktes. 193...

124. Sextett der Genien. 1937.   125. Bühnenlandschaft. 1937.

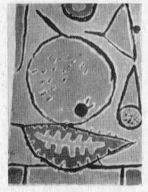

126. Bilderbogen. 1937.   127. Coelin-Frucht. 1938.   128. Park bei L (-uzern). 1938.

121. Oriental Garden.   122. Early Chill.   123. Revolution of the Viaduct.
124. Sextet of Spirits.   125. Stage Landscape.
126. Picture Page.   127. Azure Fruit.   128. Park near L (-ucerne).

276

129. Rote Weste. 1938.

130. Timider Brutaler. 1938.

131. Nach rechts nach links. 1938.

132. Zerbrochener Schlüssel. 1938.

133. Vorhaben (Entwurf). 1938.

134. Tänze vor Angst. 1938.

135. Das Fräulein vom Sport. 1938.

136. Werbeblatt·der Komiker. 1938.

129. Red Waistcoat.   130. Brutal but timid.   131. To Right and Left.
132. Broken Key.   133. Intention.
134. Dancing for Fear.   135. Miss Sport.   136. Poster for Comedians.

138. Reicher Hafen. 1938.

137. Die Vase. 1938.

140. Insula Dulcamara. 1938.

139. Der Graue und die Küste. 1938

141. Früchte auf Blau. 1938.

142. Rausch. 1939.

143. Daemonie. 1939.

137. The Vase.   138. Rich Harbour.
139. The grey Man and the Coast.   140. Insula Dulcamara.   141. Fruits on blue.
142. Intoxication.   143. Possessed.

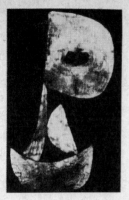

144. Ernste Miene. 1939.

145. Unterwassergarten. 1939.

146. Wachsamer Engel. 1939.

147. La Belle Jardinière. 1939.

148. Kerzen-Flammen. 1939.

149. Heilige aus einem Fenster. 1940.

150. Assel im Gehege. 1940.

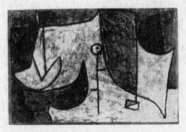

151. Stilleben am Schalttag. 1940.

144. Stern Visage.   145. Underwater Garden.   146. Guardian Angel.
147. La Belle Jardinière.   148. Candle and Flames.   149. Stained-glass Saint.
150. Woodlouse in Enclosure.   151. Still-life on Leap Day.

152. Alea jacta. 1940.   153. Gefangen. 1940.   154. Paukenspieler. 1940.

155. Frau in Tracht. 1940.   156. Flora am Felsen. 1940.   157. Matrose. 1940.

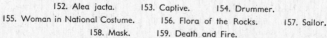

158. Maske. 1940.   159. Tod und Feuer. 1940.

152. Alea jacta.   153. Captive.   154. Drummer.
155. Woman in National Costume.   156. Flora of the Rocks.   157. Sailor.
158. Mask.   159. Death and Fire.

Klee's Writings

At a very early age Klee felt the need to note down the reflections inspired by his experiments and by his artistic creations. At first he confided them to his *Diary*, which he began in 1898 and in which amongst other matters, he narrates the events of his life, tells of his love affairs, of his friendships, of his efforts to impress people, of his enthusiasms and of his drinking bouts. This *Diary*, which allows us to trace his intellectual, moral and artistic evolution up to 1918, has recently been published by his son Felix (Europa Verlag, Zürich, 1957). It is an exceptionally interesting document.

From November 1911 until December 1912, Klee contributed articles on artistic and musical life in the Bavarian capital to the review *Die Alpen*, published in Berne.

In 1912, he translated into German an article by Robert Delaunay on *Light* (Uber das Licht), which the review *Der Sturm* published in Berlin in 1913, in its January number (No. 144/145, Vol. 3).

In 1918 he began to write Creative Confession (*Schöpferische Konfession*), the first of a series of five essays; they are mostly very brief but full of happy, stimulating formulations and, apart from Klee's own art, explain a great deal of Modern Art generally. Creative Confession appeared in 1920 in the *Tribune der Kunst und Zeit* (Tribune of the Times), Vol. XIII, edited by Kasimir Edschmid (publisher, Erich Reiss, Berlin). Part of it was translated into English under the title *Paul Klee*, 2nd edit., *Museum of Modern Art*, New York, 1945.

In 1923, another of Klee's essays, Ways of Studying Nature (*Wage des Natur-Studiums*), was published in *Staatliches Bauhaus, Weimar, 1919–1923*. Two years later, Albert Langen, Munich, published in the *Bauhausbucher* (No. 2) (Bauhaus Books), the Padagogische Skizzenbuch, an extract from lectures which Klee was giving at the Bauhaus. An English edition was published in 1944 in New York by the Nierendorf Gallery, under the title *Pedagogical Sketch Book* (translation by Sibyl Peech).

In 1928, the Bauhaus review (No. 2/3) published *Precise Experiments in the Realm of Art*, parts of which were reproduced in English under the title *Paul Klee Speaks in the Baushaus 1919–1928, Museum of Modern Art*, New York, 1938.

A lecture *Uber die Moderne Kunst* (On Modern Art) which Klee gave in 1924 at the Jena Museum and which is particularly important, was published only in 1945 by Benteli, Berne-Bümpliz. The English translation by Paul Findlay, entitled *On Modern Art*, with an introduction by Herbert Read, was published in 1937 by Faber and Faber, London, whilst a "French adaptation" by Pierre Algaux was published in Brussels in 1948 (Editions de la Connaissance).

Like the four preceding essays, the Jena Lecture has just been reproduced in the book *Das bildnerische Denken* (The Thought of the Plastic Artist), which also contains the complete text of the lectures delivered by Klee at the Bauhaus from 1921 to 1922. This profusely illustrated work (edited by Jürg Spiller and published by Benno Schwabe & Co., Basle Stuttgart, 1956) demonstrates in the clearest possible way the carefully thought out, circumspect nature of Klee's creative process and with what discrimination he employed the different means the artist uses to express himself.

Klee also wrote:

A reply to an enquiry *Uber den Wert der Kritik* (On the value of Criticism) published in the review *Der Ararat* No. 2, Publisher Goltz, Munich, 1921.

An article on *W. Kandinsky* in the catalogue of the *Jubilaumsausstellung zum 60. Geburstag von W. Kandinsky* (Jubilee Exhibition for the 60th birthday of W. Kandinsky), Arnold Gallery, Dresden, 1926.

An article on Emil Nolde in *Festschrift zum 60. Geburstag von E. Nolde*, Neue Kunst Fides, Dresden, 1927.

Eight of his poems have been reproduced by Carola Giedion-Welcker in *Poetes a l'ecart*, Benteli, Berne-Bümpliz, 1946.

Books illustrated by Klee

Klee provided illustrations for:

Candide by Voltaire (26 drawings executed in 1911), Kurt Wolff, Munich 1920. English edition: Pantheon Books, New York, 1944.

Potsdamer Platz, oder die Nächte des neuen Messias (Potsdamer Platz, or the Nights of the New Messiah) by Curt Corrinth (10 lithographs), Georg Müller, Munich, 1920.

Fifty-one of his drawings have been chosen as illustrations for *Die Lehrlinge zu Sais* (The Novices of Sais) by Novalis, Benteli, Berne-Bümpliz, 1949, English edition *The Novices of Sais* with 60 drawings, Curt Valentin, New York, 1949. A number of other works contain either a lithograph or an original engraving or reproductions of drawings or etchings.

Principal Exhibitions

Up to 1912 Klee experienced some difficulty in getting his works accepted in exhibitions and galleries. The Munich *Sezession* exhibited six of his etchings in 1906, probably as a result of the intervention of his former teacher Franz Stuck, but it rejected all his *sousverres* in 1907 and accepted only three of the six which he submitted in 1908. The Berlin *Sezession* was more accommodating, and he was admitted to its Salon in 1908 and 1909.

His first one-man exhibition of 56 works from the years 1907–1910 was held in Switzerland in 1910–1911. It was successively housed in the *Kunsthalle* in Berne, the *Kunsthaus*, Zürich, a gallery in Winterthur and the *Kunsthalle*, Basle.

In 1911, the Thannhauser Gallery in Munich, which in the same year organized the first public showing of the *Blaue Reiter*, exhibited a collection of his drawings.

In 1912, he took part in the Second Exhibition of the *Blaue Reiter* at the Goltz Gallery in Munich; in 1913, he exhibited at the *Sturm Gallery* in Berlin; in 1917, at the *dada Gallery* in Zürich.

From 1919 onwards and up to Hitler's advent to power in 1933, there were numerous Klee exhibitions in Germany. In 1919–1920, the *Kestner Gesellschaft* (Kestner Society) in Hanover organized one which included 122 of his works. A few months later, the Goltz Gallery in Munich which had just concluded a contract with the artist, sent out invitations to an even more important show of his paintings, with a catalogue of 356 works. In 1925, the same gallery presented a new collection of more than 200 works. Then Alfred Flechtheim became Paul Klee's dealer. He had already shown his works in Düsseldorf in 1920 and in 1927. Now, he showed him in Berlin: 56 works in 1928; 150 in 1929; 160 in 1930; 40 in 1931. In the same year, the *Kunstverein fur die Rheinlande und Westfalen* (Art Association for the Rhineland and Westphalia) exhibited 252 of his works in Düsseldorf.

Klee also exhibited at Frankfurt (*Zinglers Kabinett* 1919 and 1921), at Cologne (*Kunstverein* 1921), at Wiesbaden (*Nassauischer Kunstverein* 1922), in Berlin (*Galerie Fritz Gurlitt* 1919); Goldschmidt & Wallerstein 1922 and 1926; *Kronprinzenpalais* 1923; *Nationalgalerie* 1930, at Brunswick (*Landesmuseum* 1924), at Dresden (*Galerie Fides* 1924, 1926 and 1929), etc.

In 1921, the *Würthle Gallery* showed him in Vienna. In 1924, the *Anonymous Society of New York* organized his first exhibition in the United States, while his first exhibition in France took place in 1925 at the *Vavin-Raspail Gallery* (Berger and Daber). In the same year he was represented at the *Gallery Pierre* in Paris, in the first group of Surrealist painters. Three years later,

the *Gallery Le Centaure* welcomed him to Brussels. In 1929 he had another exhibition in Paris (*Gallery Bernheim Jeune*). In 1930, 63 of his works were shown at the Museum of Modern Art in New York.

From 1933 to 1940 he was no longer given an opportunity of showing his works in Germany. (However, the Nazis hung 17 of his works in the exhibition of *Degenerate Art*, which in 1937 they began to circulate in a number of German towns.) From then onwards, Klee exhibited in London (*Mayor Gallery* 1934 and 1935; *London Gallery* 1939); in Paris (*Galerie Simon*, managed by the artist's new dealer, D. H. Kahnweiler 1934–1938; *Galerie Ballay et Carre* 1938); in Berne (*Kunsthalle* 1935); at San Francisco (*Museum of Art* 1937); in New York (*Buchholtz Gallery*, Curt Valentin 1938; *Nierebdorf Galleries* 1938 and 1940) and in other cities of the United States, finally in Zurich (*Kunsthaus* 1940).

The war slowed down the rhythm of exhibitions. In Europe, under the German occupation, there was no questions of exhibitions of works by Klee. After the artist's death, however, retrospective exhibitions were organized in Switzerland—in Berne (*Kunsthalle* 1940), in Zürich (*Kunsthaus* 1940–drawings and etchings only), in Basle (*Kunsthalle* 1941). Other exhibitions, some of them retrospective, took place between 1940 and 1945 in London (*Leicester Galleries* 1914), in New York (*Bucholz & Willard Gallery* 1940, *Nierendorf Gallery* 1941 and 1942, *Museum of Modern Art* 1941, *Bucholz Gallery*, Curt Valentin 1943), in

Chicago (*Arts Club* 1941), in San Francisco (*Museum of Art* 1941), in Philadelphia (*Art Alliance* 1944), etc.

With the return of peace, Klee exhibitions increased in number. They were organized at Lucerne (*Galerie Rosengart* 1945 and 1948), in Basle (*Galerie d'Art Moderne* 1945 and 1949), in Berne (*Kunstmuseum* 1947), Zürich (*Kunsthaus* 1948), in Paris (*Galerie Colette Allendy* 1948, *Musee National d'Art Moderne* 1948; *Galerie Jeanne Bucher* 1950; *Gallerie Berggruen* 1952, 1953, 1955; *Galerie Simone Heller* 1956). There were Klee exhibitions in Munich (*Galerie Stangl* 1948; *Haus der Kunst* 1949 and 1950) in Düsseldorf (*Hetjens Museum* 1948); in Mannheim (*Städtische Kunsthalle* 1949), in Brunswick (*Galerie Otto Ralfs* 1949), in Hanover (*Kestner Gesellschaft* 1952 and 1954), and elsewhere.

Retrospective exhibitions were also held in the *Palais des Beaux-Arts* in Brussels and at the Amsterdam *Municipal Museum* 1948 and 1957, at the *National Gallery* in London 1945, at the Venice *Biennale* 1948, and in Sao Paulo 1953, as well as in a number of American cities (*Beverly Hills* 1948; *Museum of Modern Art*, New York 1949–1950; etc.). Finally the *Kunstmuseum* in Berne showed in 1956 the biggest selection of Klee's works ever shown together: 756 paintings, water-colours, pastels, drawings, etchings and sculptures.

Bibliography

The first books devoted to Klee were: the *Sturm Bilderbuch* (Sturm-Picture Book) No. 3, 1918 (15 drawings). Soon afterwards, there appeared *Paul Klee* by Hans von Wedderkop (Klinkhardt & Biermann, Leipzig, 1920, vol. 13 of the collection *Junge Kunst* (Young Art) (16 pages and 33 illustrations); *Paul Klee: Leben, Werk, Geist* (Paul Klee: Life, Works and Spirit) by Leopold Zahn (Kiepenheurer, Potsdam, 1920, 87 pages, 69 illustrations); *Kairuan, oder eine Geschichte von Maler Klee und von der Kunst dieses Zeitalters* (Kairuan, or a Tale of Klee, the Painter, and the Art of Today) by Wilhelm Hausenstein (Kurt Wolff, Munich, 1921, 134 pages, 42 illustrations). At a time when admirers of Klee were rare, these works enthusiastically stressed the importance of Klee's work and brought out the original traits in his personality. "I see no one in Germany", wrote Wedderkop "who has so many new things to say."

In 1929, Will Grohmann published *Paul Klee*, a collection of appreciations by Louis Aragon, Paul Eluard, René Crevel, Jean Lurçat, Philippe Soupault, Tristan Tzara, Roger Vitrac (Editions des Cahiers d'Art, Paris, 27 pages, 91 illustrations).

After Klee's death, Benteli, Berne, published the speeches made by Hans Bloesch and Georg Schmidt at his funeral, *Paul Klee, Reden zu seinem Todestag, 29 Juni 1940* (Paul Klee, Speeches on the Day of his Death, 29th June 1940) (18 pages, 5 illustrations).

In 1950, *Five Essays on Klee*, by Merle

Armitage, Clement Greenberg, Howard Devree, Nancy Wilson Ross and James Johnson Sweeney, were published by Duell, Sloan & Pearce, New York (18 pages, 5 illustrations).

In the same year there was published the first book which attempted to retrace the painter's evolution and to demonstrate the importance of his art: *Paul Klee, Wege bildnerischen Denkens* (The Plastic Artist's Modes of Thought), by Werner Haftmann (Prestel Verlag, Munich, 178 pages, 36 illustrations). This study was succeeded in 1952 by the English edition of *Paul Klee* by Carola Giedion-Welcker (The Viking Press, New York, 156 pages illustrated). In 1954, the same work was published in German (its original text) by Gerd Hatje, Stuttgart (204 pages, 172 illustrations). Will Grohmann's large monograph was also published in 1954: German Edition: W. Kohlhammer, Stuttgart, 447 pages, 486 illustrations; French edition: Flinker, 454 pages, 486 illustrations; English edition.

Haftmann's book is in the nature of an introduction to Klee's method. He analyses with great penetration the artist's concepts of the artist, his creative processes and the broad outlines of his evolution, basing himself on Klee's writings and his lecture notes as well as on his works.

Carola Giedion-Welcker's book is at once more brief, more concise and more solidly based on historical information. Full of intelligence and authority, it highlights all the essentials. It sets out the principal problems which preoccupied the painter or with which we are faced when confronted with his art; it interprets his paintings in a subtle, convincing manner. The book also includes a large number of reproductions some of which bring Klee's painting into eloquent juxtaposition with works of Picasso, Braque, Kandinsky, Mirò and others.

Will Grohamm, who knew the artist personally for some twenty years, and to whom Klee himself suggested, in 1935 that he should write a monograph, produced a monumental work divided into three parts. Making use of Klee's Diary and Letters as well as of his own memories, he begins with a detailed biography of the artist. He then makes a lengthy and penetrating study of the different aspects of his art, describes its genesis and explains its scope. Finally, he discusses Klee's work as a teacher and summarizes both his theoretical discourses and his lectures. The work is abundantly illustrated. The French edition contains (in addition to Grohmann's text) a preface by Henri Michaux (*Aventures de Lignes* (Adventures with Line)) and a graphological portrait by Ania Teillard.

For some years there have been available a large number of books offering a choice of black and white or coloured reproductions with introductions of varying lengths. They are given below in chronological order.

René Crevel, *Paul Klee*, Gallimard, Paris, 1930, Coll. Peintres Nouveaux (63 pages, 37 illustrations); Will Grohmann, *Handzeichnungen* (Drawings) 1921–1930, Müller & I. Kiepenheuer, Berlin, 1934 (30 pages, 74 illustrations), English Edition: The

Drawings of Paul Klee, Curt Valentin, New York, 1944 (20 pages, 73 illustrations), New German edition, Müller & Kiepenheuer, Bergen, 1948; Karl Nierendorf, *Paul Klee, Paintings, Watercolours*, 1913 to 1939, Oxford University Press, New York, 1941, Curt Valentin, New York, 1945 (26 pages, 45 illustrations), 2nd edition *Museum of Modern Art*, New York, 1947; Georg Schmidt, *Ten Reproductions in Facsimile of Paintings by Paul Klee*, Wittenborn, New York, 1946 (10 pages, 10 illustrations); German edition: Holbein-Verlag, Basle, 1946; Georg Schmidt, *Ten Facsimile Reproductions of Works in Watercolour and Tempera*, Holbein Verlag, Basle, 1948 (14 pages, 10 illustrations), Bruno Alfieri, *Paul Klee*, Instituto Tipografico Editoriale, Venice, 1948 (25 pages, 6 illustrations); Hans Friedrich Geist, *Paul Klee*, Hauswedell, Hamburg, 1948 (46 pages, illustrated); Felix Klee, *Paul Klee, 22 Zeichnungen* (22 drawings), Eidos Presse, Stuttgart, 1948 (4 pages, 22 illustrations); Herbert Read, *Klee* (1879–1940), Faber & Faber, London, 1948 (24 pages, 11 illustrations); Douglas Cooper, *Paul Klee*, Penguin Books, Harmondsworth, 1949 (16 pages, 32 illustrations); Daniel-Henry Kahnweiler, *Klee*, Braun, Paris, and E. S. Harmann, New York (Coll. Palettes), 1950 (32 pages, 24 illustrations); Will Grohmann, *Paul Klee, Handzeichnungen*, Insel-Verlag, Wiesbaden, 1951 (13 pages, 40 illustrations); Pierre Courthion, *Klee*, Fernand Hazan, Paris, 1953, Bibliotèque Aldine des Arts (6 pages, 20 illustrations); Will Grohmann, *Paul Klee, aquarelles et dessins* (Paul Klee, watercolours and drawings), Bergguen, Paris, 1953 (21 pages, illustrated); Georg Schmidt, *Engel bringt das Gewunschte* (An Angel makes the Wish come true), Woldemar Klein, Baden-Baden, 1953 (12 illustrations with commentary); A. Forge, *Paul Klee*, Faber & Faber, London, 1954 (24 pages, 72 illustrations); Marcel Brion, *Klee*, Aimery Somogy, Paris, 1955 (23 pages, 72 illustrations); Joseph-Emile Muller, *Klee, Magic Squares* (10 pages, 20 illustrations); Georg Schmidt, *Klee, 10 Farbenlichtdrucke nach Werben der Sammlung Doetsch-Benziger, Basel* (Klee, 10 coloured prints of works in the Doetsch-Benziger Collection, Basle), Phoebus-Verlag, Basle, 1956.

Index of Works Reproduced

Entries are listed under the year in which they were produced. The numbers in brackets following the titles are those given by the artist in the inventory of his work. The figures in italic following the collection sources refer to the pages on which the reproductions appear; the bold figures are the numbers of the illustrations in the *Catalogue of Principal Works*. Colour plates are indicated thus*.

288

1928

Alte Stadt Ueberblick. (Qu.8)
Old Town—Panorama. Water-colour on paper: 11$\frac{3}{8}$″ × 8$\frac{5}{8}$″.
Richard Doetsch-Benziger Collection, Basle. **72**

Italienische Stadt. (P.6)
Italian Town. Water-colour, paper on cardboard: 13$\frac{3}{8}$″ × 9$\frac{1}{4}$″.
F. K. Collection, Berne. **73**

Grosser Circus. (L.2)
Big Circus. Chinese ink.
Private Collection, Berne. *91*

Obertöne. (K.9)
Overtones. Chinese ink: 16$\frac{1}{8}$″ × 10$\frac{1}{4}$″.
Private Collection, Berne. *111*

Kleine Seenot. (L.3).
Slight Danger at Sea. Chinese ink: 18″ × 12$\frac{7}{8}$″.
Klee-Stiftung, Berne. *84*

Alte Stadt und Brücke. (F.10)
*Old Town and Bridge. Distemper on sacking: 4$\frac{1}{2}$″ × 16$\frac{5}{8}$″.
Richard Doetsch-Benziger Collection, Basle. *122–23*

Ein Blatt aus dem Städtebuch. (N.6)
*A Leaf from the Town Records. Oil on chalk, paper on wood: 16$\frac{5}{8}$″ × 12$\frac{3}{8}$″.
Kunstmuseum, Basle. *106*

Eingezäuntes. (Qu.4)
*Cloisonné. Oil on paper, stuck on wood and plaster: 8$\frac{3}{4}$″ × 11$\frac{1}{8}$″.
Siegfried Rosengart Collection, Lucerne. *122*

1929

Angst hinter Fenster. (3 H.28)
*Fear behind the Curtain. Water-colour: 9$\frac{5}{8}$″ × 12$\frac{3}{8}$″.
Rosengart Gallery, Lucerne. *107*

Die Stelle der Zwillinge. (3 H.21)
*The Twins' Place. Water-colour, paper on cardboard: 10$\frac{3}{4}$″ × 12″.
Klee-Stiftung, Berne. *135*

Rechnender Greis. (S.9)
Old Man calculating. Etching. *121*

Belichtetes Blatt. (OE.4)
*Illuminated Leaf. Water-colour and pen, paper on cardboard: 12″ × 9″.
Klee-Stiftung, Berne. *134*

Die Sonne streift die Ebene. (M.4)
The Sun sweeps the Plain. Water-colour, paper on cardboard: 14$\frac{7}{8}$″ × 9$\frac{3}{4}$″.
Klee-Stiftung, Berne. **74**

Nichtkomponiertes im Raum. (C.4)
Uncomposed Objects in Space. Pen-drawing and water-colour: 12$\frac{5}{8}$″ × 9$\frac{7}{8}$″.
Private Collection, Berne. **75**

Ein Kreuzfahrer. (T.2)
A Crusader. Water-colour on paper: 17$\frac{1}{8}$″ × 11″.
F. C. Schang Collection, New York. **76**

Hauptweg und Nebenwege. (R.10)
Highway and Byways. Oil on canvas: 32$\frac{5}{8}$″ × 26$\frac{3}{8}$″.
Madame Werner Vowinckel Collection, Munich. **77**

Clown. (D.3). Oil on canvas with Meuden white: 26$\frac{3}{4}$″ × 19$\frac{5}{8}$″.
Curt Valentin Collection, New York. **78**

Irrende Seele. (3 h.11)
Wandering Soul. Water-colour and pen-drawing: 9$\frac{1}{2}$″ × 14$\frac{1}{8}$″.
Private Collection, Berne. **79**

Vor dem Schnee. (3 h.19)
Before the Snow. Water-colour, paper on cardboard: 13$\frac{1}{4}$″ × 15$\frac{3}{8}$″.
Private Collection, Berne. **80**

Kirche und Schloss. (M.7)
Church and Castle. Pen-drawing.
F. K. Collection, Berne. *120*

Nekropolis. (S.1)
Necropolis. Gouache: 15″ × 9$\frac{7}{8}$″.
D. H. Kahnweiler, Paris. **81**

Monument im Fruchtland. (N.1)
*Monument in fertile Land. Water-colour, paper on cardboard: 18$\frac{1}{8}$″ × 12″.
Klee-Stiftung, Berne. *137*

Gemischtes Wetter. (3 h.43)
*Mixed Weather. Oil and water-colour on muslin: 19$\frac{1}{4}$″ × 16$\frac{1}{8}$″.
F. K. Collection, Berne. *126*

Physiognomische Genesis. (C.5)
*Genesis of the Physiognomy. Water-colour: 12$\frac{5}{8}$″ × 9$\frac{3}{4}$″.
F. K. Collection, Berne. *123*

Wolke über Bäumen. (N.15)
Cloud above the Trees. Crayon: $8\frac{3}{8}''\times25''$.
Klee-Stiftung, Berne. 144

Schwerbefruchtet. (Qu.10)
Heavily pregnant. Crayon. 133

Am und im See. (N.16)
On and in the Lake. Crayon: $9\frac{1}{2}''\times24\frac{1}{2}''$.
Klee-Stiftung, Berne. 138

Gemischte Siesta. (N.20)
Confused Siesta. Crayon: $6\frac{7}{8}''\times25\frac{1}{8}''$.
Klee-Stiftung, Berne. 150

Bald marschieren mehr. (R.13)
More will be marching soon. Crayon: $12\frac{5}{8}''\times7''$.
Klee-Stiftung, Berne. 146

Angst. (U.2)
Fear. Oil and water-colour, covered with wax, on canvas: $19\frac{5}{8}''\times21\frac{5}{8}''$.
Nelson A. Rockefeller Collection, New York. **107**

Botanisches Theater. (U.19)
Botanical Theatre. Oil and water-colour on canvas: $19\frac{5}{8}''\times26\frac{3}{8}''$.
Private Collection, Berne. **108**

Blühendes. (T.19)
Blossom. Oil on canvas: $31\frac{7}{8}''\times31\frac{1}{2}''$.
Dr. E. Friedrich Collection, Zurich. **109**

Trauernd. (8)
Mourning. Water-colour, paper on cardboard: $19\frac{1}{4}''\times12\frac{5}{8}''$.
Klee-Stiftung, Berne. **110**

1935
Spiel auf dem Wasser. (3)
Game on the Water. Crayon: $7''\times10\frac{5}{8}''$.
Klee-Stiftung, Berne. 199

Grobgeschnittener Kopf. (K.12)
Roughhewn Head. Wash: $13''\times8\frac{1}{4}''$.
F. C. Schang Collection, New York. 147

Gartenfigur 'zur Warnung'. (12)
Warning. Crayon: $11''\times7''$.
Klee-Stiftung, Berne. 135

Ausdrucks-Leier. (14)
Expressive Lyre. Crayon: $10\frac{7}{8}''\times7''$.
Klee-Stiftung, Berne. 148

Rindenkultur. (P.5)
Bark Culture. *Sous-verre*: $11''\times7\frac{1}{4}''$.
F. K. Collection, Berne. 155

Tor zum verlassenen Garten. (L.18)
*Gate of the deserted Garden. Gouache: $12\frac{5}{8}''\times17\frac{3}{4}''$.
Private Collection, Berne. 206

Der gefundene Ausweg. (N.18)
*The Way-out at last. Water-colour on paper: $12\frac{5}{8}''\times18\frac{7}{8}''$.
F. K. Collection, Berne. 202

Zwei-Frucht-Landschaft II. (L.9)
*Two Fruit Landscape II. Water-colour: $9\frac{1}{2}''\times13''$.
F. K. Collection, Berne. 209

Möblierte Arktis. (M.1)
*Furnished Arctic. Gouache: $11\frac{1}{4}''\times18\frac{1}{4}''$.
Rosengart Gallery, Lucerne. 216

W-geweihtes Kind. (K.11)
Child consecrated to W (Woe). Gouache and oil: $5\frac{7}{8}''\times9''$.
Albright Art Gallery, Buffalo. **111**

Dame Dämon. (P.15)
Dame Demon. Distemper and oil on canvas: $59\frac{1}{2}''\times39\frac{3}{4}''$.
Klee-Stiftung, Berne. **112**

Zeichen auf dem Feld. (M.17)
Signs in the Field. Water-colour. **113**

1936
Betroffene Stadt.
Stricken Town. Oil on plaster: $17\frac{7}{8}''\times13\frac{7}{8}''$.
Dr. W. Loeffler Collection, Zurich. **114**

*Caligula. (4). Water-colour on paper: $19\frac{1}{4}''\times9\frac{1}{2}''$.
F. K. Collection, Berne. 221

1937
Schwanenteich. (V.1)
Pond with Swans. Colour mixed with black gum: $18\frac{7}{8}''\times16\frac{1}{2}''$.
Mrs. John Rockefeller Collection, New York. 170

Ach, aber ach. (U.1)
Oh! But Oh! Colour mixed with gum and black water-colour: $7\frac{1}{8}''\times11\frac{3}{8}''$.
Private Collection, Berne. 163

Neu angelegter Garten. (K.7)
*Newly laid-out Garden. Gouache on plaster: $9\frac{1}{2}''\times12\frac{1}{4}''$.
Private Collection, Berne. 212

Index of Persons